The Knights Templar

PILGRIM SITES
at the time of the Crusades

Mediterranean

GALILEE

Safad

Acre

Capernaum
Table of the Lord
Bethsaida

Haifa

Cana

Magdalon

Sea of Galilee

Mount Carmel

Sephoria

Tiberias

'Atlit

Nazareth

Mount Tabor

Nain

SAMARIA

Caesarea

Baisan

Dothan

Samaria

Nablus

Jacob's Well

River Jordan

Jaffa

Arimathea

JUDAEA

Lydda

Ramla

Mountjoy

Mount Quarantene

Gardens of Abraham

Cave of John the Baptist

Jericho

Spring of Emmaus

Tomb of the Virgin

Red Cistern

Baptism of Christ

Jerusalem

Church of the Ascension

Tomb of David

Bethany

Ascalon

Bethlehem

Shepherds Fields

Dead Sea

Bethgibelin

Hebron

Tomb of Lot

0   30 km
0   20 miles

The Knights Templar

The History and Myths of the Legendary Military Order

SEAN MARTIN

THUNDER'S MOUTH PRESS
NEW YORK

THE KNIGHTS TEMPLAR
The History and Myths of the Legendary Military Order

Published by
Thunder's Mouth Press
An Imprint of Avalon Publishing Group Inc.
245 West 17th St., 11th Floor
New York, NY 10011

AVALON
publishing group incorporated

Copyright © 2004 by Sean Martin

First published in the UK by Pocket Essentials, March 2004
First Thunder's Mouth Press edition December 2004

Library of Congress Cataloging-in-Publication Data is available.

ISBN 1-56025-645-1

9   8   7   6   5   4   3   2   1

Book design by Avocet Typeset, Chilton, Aylesbury, Bucks
Printed in Canada on recycled paper

Distributed by Publishers Group West

'What is history, but a fable agreed upon?'

Napoleon Bonaparte

Acknowledgements

Thanks are due to Nicholas Mark Harding, for lending me certain not-so-ancient tomes on this occasion, Mike Paine for the usual moral support, and Richard Leigh, for his advice relating to matters discussed in Chapter 4.

Contents

Introduction:
The Temple and the Myth

On the morning of 21 January 1793, the French king, Louis XVI, was led out into the Place de la Concord in Paris to face execution. He stepped up onto the platform where the guillotine had been erected, and turned to address the huge crowd who had come to watch him die. He announced that he forgave the revolutionary council who had voted for his death, and then gave himself over to the executioner. The blade fell at 10:15. The executioner held Louis' decapitated head up by the hair to show that the king was dead. What happened next, according to some sources,[1] took the crowd by surprise: a man jumped up onto the platform and dipped his fingers in the dead king's blood. He held his hand aloft and shouted 'Jacques de Molay, thus you are avenged!' The crowd cheered, understanding the reference to the last Templar Grand Master, who was burned as a relapsed heretic in 1314; the long-held popular rumour that one day the Templars would have their revenge on the French monarchy – which had brought the Order down on dubious charges of heresy, blasphemy and sodomy – seemed to have come true. Indeed, speculation was rife that the Templars were among the instigators of the revolution that had swept through

France in 1789, ultimately claiming the lives of Louis and his queen, Marie Antoinette.

Modern historians would scoff at such a notion, but it certainly illustrates the unique hold the Knights Templar have had on the European imagination ever since they emerged from obscurity in the late 1120s. They have been seen as heroic soldier-monks guarding pilgrims to the Holy Land during the Crusades, defenders of Holy Church who fought alongside Richard the Lionheart. Their critics – in their own time, usually annalists and commentators from rival monastic orders – accused them of the sins of pride and arrogance, and were deeply suspicious of the air of secrecy that hung over the Order like a veil. To Walter Scott, they were evil, and he made them the villains of *Ivanhoe*. Modern historians have tried to show that the Templars were a highly efficient military organisation made up largely of illiterates who were in reality very ordinary; their achievements were to be the creation of the first standing army in Europe since the days of the Roman Empire, and – as the first bankers in the West – the mediaeval organisation that did most to pave the way for modern capitalism.

Those of a more speculative cast of mind – and there have been many over the centuries – have seen the Order variously as an esoteric brotherhood, hungry for forbidden knowledge; apostates involved in diabolic practices who were the witches' next of kin; a mysterious political entity that has guided world affairs since their suppression, clandestinely directing world events from behind the scenes; and renegade Christians who supported and sheltered heretics, forged links with occult groups in the Arab world and who discovered the Turin Shroud, the Ark of the Covenant and the Holy Grail.

Books about the Templars tend to fall into two camps: what could be termed orthodox and speculative. The former camp is represented by academics such as Malcolm Barber, whose studies *The New Knighthood* and *The Trial of the Templars* are critically acclaimed and are the books one should consult if one is seeking a comprehensive treatment of Templar history. The latter camp of speculative writers has spawned a thriving industry of books containing a multitude of theories ranging from the plausible to the risible. In France – where there is a vast literature on the Templars – the Order holds a position similar to that of Glastonbury in England, a sort of historical *tabula rasa* onto which almost anything can be projected.

This book will trace the Templar story, from its beginnings in the early twelfth century, through to the suppression of the Order by the Pope in 1312 and the execution of Jacques de Molay two years later. The myths surrounding them will be examined in a later chapter. Whether or not there is any truth to them is, of course, another matter.

The Rise of the Order
of the Temple
(1119–45)

The Order of Poor Knights of the Temple of Solomon, more commonly known as the Order of the Temple or The Knights Templar, was founded by the French nobleman Hugues de Payen in around the year 1119 in Jerusalem. The Holy City, back in Christian hands ever since the First Crusade twenty years previously, was the main destination for pilgrims from Europe. They came in their droves, unaware of the dangers that lay ahead – the roads around Jerusalem were notorious for the bands of robbers that haunted them, preying on the travellers to the Holy Places. Sometimes these robbers were Saracens; sometimes they were lapsed crusaders. To counter this threat, Hugues de Payen gathered a group of nine knights together to protect the pilgrims.

Hugues and his brothers did not look like the knights of popular imagination. They had no money, wore clothes that were donated to them and suffered from a constant shortage of new recruits and equipment in the early years of their existence. Yet by 1129, at the Council of Troyes, the Templars had become almost overnight the heroes of Christian Europe, and between 1139 and 1145, the Pope issued a series of three papal bulls that gave the Templars almost total power, making them answerable to none save the pontiff himself. It was one of the most remarkable turnarounds of the Middle Ages, if not of all European history.

If we are to understand why and how the Templars rose to such prominence so quickly after such apparently humble beginnings, we need to take a look at the background to the Jerusalem in which they found themselves at their inception, and trace the history of the city itself, right back to the original Temple of Solomon.

The First Temple

The original temple in Jerusalem was the Temple of Solomon, built by the great king around the year 950 BC. The site – known ever since as the Temple Mount or the Temple platform – had been chosen by his father, King David, who recognised it as the spot on which Abraham had prepared his son Isaac for sacrifice.

Abraham is thought to have lived 18 centuries before Christ, and was one of the founding fathers of the Jewish nation. His attempt to sacrifice Isaac symbolised both his obedience to God and his fear of Him. As Abraham raised the knife to kill his child, God spoke and ordered him to stay his hand; Abraham complied, and God was pleased. He promised Abraham that He would 'shower blessings' on him and make his people, the Jews, 'as many as the stars of heaven and the grains of sand on the seashore'.[2] The spot of the attempted sacrifice came to represent, for the Jews, their unbreakable bond with God.

In addition, the Temple was to house the Ark of the Covenant, which was constructed to keep the stone tablets on which were written the Ten Commandments that Moses brought down from Mount Sinai. Like the story of Abraham and Isaac, the Commandments were tangible proof of the Jews' covenant with the Almighty.

Solomon was reputedly the wisest of men, and his reign marks a high point of the Jewish nation; the Temple that he constructed in Jerusalem was said to have profound wisdom embodied in its architecture, and was a place of awe, pilgrimage and devotion. But it was not to last. Israel was occupied by successive invasions from the East, first by the Assyrians, and then, in 586 BC, by the Chaldeans. Their king, Nebuchadnezzar, ordered that the Temple be destroyed and the Jewish people taken into slavery at Babylon. The Chaldeans were, in turn, ousted by the Persians, whose king, Cyrus, allowed the Jews to return home in 515 BC and rebuild the temple.

Political uncertainty in the second century BC led Israel to appeal for protection from Rome. What initially started as diplomatic intervention became, by the time of Julius Caesar's visit in 47 BC, occupation. This in turn led to much dissent and the formation of groups opposed to Roman rule. There was a general expectation of a Messiah, who would arrive and liberate the Jewish people once and for all from the tyranny of occupation. Some believed this to be Jesus, whose followers were outlawed and persecuted, being seen as agitators and, in some cases, terrorists. In AD 70, the Jews revolted. The Romans retaliated brutally, crushing the uprising; the Temple was destroyed for a second time. In 134, there was another uprising, led by Simeon ben-Koseba, who, according to the Rabbi Akiba, really was the long-awaited Messiah. This was also crushed, leading to the Jews being banned from entering Jerusalem at all.

By the early fourth century, Jerusalem was becoming a Holy City for a second faith, that of the new religion of Christianity. In 312, the Roman Emperor Constantine converted, and he ordered that churches be built over the site of Christ's birth in Bethlehem, and those of his Crucifixion and Resurrection in Jerusalem; the latter church became known as the Church of the Holy Sepulchre. However, Constantine's nephew and successor, Julian the Apostate, did not share his uncle's beliefs, and the Empire returned to paganism. In a blatant attempt to antagonise Christians, Julian began to rebuild the Temple (not that he had any time for the Jews, who were persecuted with equal zeal). The project did not progress smoothly, and was abandoned upon Julian's death in 363. Jerusalem seemed destined never to have another Temple.

The Temple and the Mosque

With its administration creaking, the Roman Empire divided into two in the fourth century – the western half would still be ruled by Rome, while the eastern half had Byzantium as its capital. When Rome was overrun by the Visigoths in 410, Jerusalem became one of many jewels in the Byzantine crown. The Temple Mount became a rubbish tip.

In 638, Jerusalem surrendered to the Caliph Omar, and the city fell into Muslim hands. Since its founding by the

Prophet Muhammad with the *hijrah* of 622, when the Prophet migrated from Mecca to Medina and thus the Muslim calendar began, Islam had spread rapidly throughout the Middle East. The Byzantines seemed powerless to stop its progress, and retreated north. Jerusalem was sacred to Muslims, in particular the Temple Mount area, as it was the site of the Prophet's ascension to heaven. Upon his entry into Jerusalem, Omar had gone there to pray, and resolved to build the al-Aqsa mosque on the site. Towards the end of the seventh century, a second, even more impressive, mosque was built on the Temple Mount, the Dome of the Rock. Jerusalem was further than ever from Christian hands.

The First Crusade

Islam continued to impinge upon Christian Europe, with most of the Mediterranean and the Iberian peninsula falling under Muslim control during the seventh and eighth centuries. By the middle of the eleventh century, a new Islamic threat had emerged, from the Seljuk Turks. Originally from central Asia, they had moved inexorably westwards, conquering Baghdad and converting to Islam in the process. They had Byzantium in their sights, and in 1071 defeated the imperial army at Manzikert in Armenia. Within a decade, they had also taken Nicea and controlled the whole of Asia Minor. The Byzantine empire was now solely comprised of its lands west of the Bosphorous, and it was to the West that the Byzantine emperor Alexius looked for help to stave off certain annihilation.

In the spring of 1095, a delegation arrived at the Council of Piacenza in northern Italy. Although the eastern and western churches had split decisively in 1054, the Pope, Urban II, had made conciliatory moves towards Constantinople by rescinding Alexius' excommunication, and it was therefore with some hope that the eastern delegation appealed to the council. Its plea for help did not fall on deaf ears. Urban called for a meeting of bishops to address the problem, to be held that November in Clermont.

On Tuesday 27 November 1095, after a week-long ecclesiastical conference in the cathedral, Urban addressed a huge crowd outside the walls of Clermont. He called on those assembled to desist from fighting one another, internecine warfare having dogged Europe ever since the sack of Rome in 410; he called instead that their energies be better spent fighting the infidel in the East, and returning Jerusalem into the arms of Mother Church. The crowd was ecstatic, with cries of '*Deus lo volt*!' – 'God wills it!' – echoing from the city walls. A bishop and a cardinal immediately knelt before Urban and begged to join the campaign. The First Crusade had begun.

After arriving in Constantinople in late 1096, the crusaders marched south, taking Nicea in June of the following year. Edessa and Antioch both fell in 1098, and the crusaders finally arrived outside the walls of the Holy City on 7 June 1099. Jerusalem finally fell on 15 July after a ferocious bloodbath. It was the first time it had been in Christian hands for 461 years. One of the Crusade's leaders, Godfroi de Bouillon – after refusing to be called king on the grounds that only Christ had the right to that title –

was proclaimed Defender of the Holy Sepulchre, and the Latin Kingdom of Jerusalem was thus established. In Europe, it became known as Outremer – the land beyond the seas.

The New Knighthood

After the victory of the First Crusade, most of the surviving crusaders returned to Europe, leaving Baldwin de Boulogne – Godfroi having died unexpectedly in the autumn of 1100 – to assume the title of the first King of Jerusalem. His domain stretched south to the Red Sea, and north as far as Beirut. Above that lay the County of Tripoli, ruled by Raymond de Saint-Gilles, Count of Toulouse. North of Tripoli was the Principality of Antioch, whose ruler was Bohemond of Taranto. The two remaining Christian kingdoms were the County of Edessa to the north-east – the first Latin kingdom to be established by the crusaders, in 1098 – and Cilician Armenia to the north-west, in what is now Turkey. Outremer, being as it was a collection of small, largely coastal kingdoms ruled by allied European nobles, was largely modelled on the feudal system that had dominated Europe since the late Dark Ages.

After the fall of the Roman Empire in the West, Europe was ravaged by successive waves of invaders: the Saracens and Magyars from the east; the Vikings from the north. In addition, kingdoms were constantly engaged in squabbles with one another, and this uncertain political climate gave rise to what became known – from the sixteenth century onwards – as the feudal system. None of the kingdoms of Europe had a centralised power base and, as a result, monarchs were largely powerless to protect their people. In order to secure some form of protection and to feed his family, a man would have to offer his services to the local landowner. With no such thing as a standing army, the landowner would always need to call upon men to fight to protect his dominions. Thus, the man swore loyalty to the lord, and became known as his vassal. Vassalage required that the man swear an oath of loyalty to his lord and be on call to fight for him whenever the need arose. In return, the lord would provide the vassal with land (or sometimes the income from ecclesiastical institutions), which would feed the vassal's family and also bring in revenue to the lord's exchequer from taxes levied on the vassal's land.

It was against this background that knights began to emerge. The lord–vassal system may have had its origins in the old Roman practice of commendation, in which a soldier would pledge service to an officer of superior rank in return for a reward to be decided by the officer. Usually it took the form of a grant of land, which was known as a benefice. European monarchs, such as Charlemagne, began to adopt this practice, and gave their best warriors grants of land. The warriors in turn would take on vassals to work the land on their behalf, thus leaving them essentially free to develop their military and equestrian skills. However, although both knight and vassal were made to swear oaths of loyalty to their lord, it was possible for them to move on to serve another lord if the protection provided proved to be inadequate, or if the lord in question was deposed or killed. In most cases, though, the relationship between lord, knight and vassal became hereditary.

The crusaders who stormed Jerusalem in the summer of 1099 were a mixture of lords, knights and vassals, and all had been promised full remission of their earthly sins for taking part in the Crusade, or pilgrimage, as it was called. The lure of remission also proved an enticing prospect for other, less savoury characters. This latter group included convicted criminals and excommunicates, who used the Crusade as a means of escaping punishment back home. Thus, when the city was safely in Frankish hands, most of the surviving crusaders returned to Europe, having achieved their objectives in taking the Holy City and also having absolved themselves of all wrongdoing. Baldwin then faced the problem of ruling a kingdom with no standing army to protect it.

Despite the fact that all the major cities and ports of Outremer were in Christian hands, the kingdom's roads were anything but secure. Even when under Muslim control, the Holy Land had continued to attract Christian pilgrims, and now that a Christian king sat on the throne of Jerusalem, they came in even greater numbers. The sites they visited were known simply as The Holy Places, and were scattered throughout the Kingdom: Sephoria was where the Virgin had spent her childhood; in Bethlehem, there was the site of the Nativity; the River Jordan was the scene of Christ's baptism by John the Baptist (whose cave dwelling was nearby); while various locales around the Sea of Galilee were witnesses to Christ's ministry. Mount Tabor was the site of the Transfiguration, while the road from Jerusalem to Jericho was the location of the Good Samaritan's charity.

However, the pilgrims were never safe once they were outside the walls of Jerusalem, as attacks by bands of Saracen robbers were frequent. Even as early as 1106, there were reports of trouble. A Russian abbot by the name of Daniel wrote of his visit to the tomb of St George at Lydda that year:

> 'And there are many springs here; travellers rest by the water but with great fear, for it is a deserted place and nearby is the town of Ascalon from which Saracens sally forth and kill travellers on these roads. There is a great fear too, going up from that place into the hills.'[3]

But that was nothing compared to Galilee:

> 'This place is very dreadful and dangerous ... many tall palm trees stand about the town like a dense forest. This place is terrible and difficult of access for here live fierce pagan Saracens who attack travellers at the fords.'[4]

Thirteen years later, things had got even worse. At Easter 1119, a group of 700 pilgrims was attacked by Saracens on the road to the River Jordan; 300 were killed and 60 carried off into slavery. Later that year, the forces of Roger, Bohemond II of Antioch's regent, were ambushed and killed at the Field of Blood. This led to a flurry of requests for further aid from the West, and a council of Church leaders met in Nablus in January 1120 to address the issue.

At the time that Roger and his men met their fate on the

Field of Blood, Baldwin's successor, Baldwin II, had been on the throne of Jerusalem for a year. It is thought that at some point during 1119 he granted an audience to two French noblemen, Hugues de Payen from Champagne and Godfrey de St Omer from Picardy. Together with seven other knights, they proposed to guard the pilgrims as they made their way to and from the Holy Places. But they would not do so as regular knights – they would live as a small monastic community, following the rule of St Augustine. Baldwin liked the idea. Manpower had always been an issue in Outremer and the fact that Hugues and his brethren were prepared to live as monks meant that they would be, in theory, more dependable than some of the rabble who had taken part in the First Crusade. The king approved the plan and, on Christmas Day, Hugues and Godfrey swore vows of poverty, chastity and obedience before Baldwin and Warmund of Picquigny, the Patriarch of Jerusalem, in the Church of the Holy Sepulchre, and Baldwin gave them quarters at the al-Aqsa mosque on the Temple platform. The Order of Poor Knights of the Temple of Solomon, the Order of the Temple, The Knights Templar, was born.

Within weeks of the founding of their order, the Templars were introduced to the clergy at the Council of Nablus. The nine knights were accepted by those present, and Hugues and his brothers began their task of policing the kingdom. The other founding knights were: Payen de Montdidier; André de Montbard; Archambaud de St Aignan, Geoffrey Bisol; two knights known only by their Christian names of Roland and Gondemar; while the ninth member remains unknown.

The Templars' first decade is their least documented. After Nablus, we can only assume that they continued to live as monks in the 'Temple of Solomon' (the crusaders' name for the al-Aqsa mosque) and to protect the pilgrims who would arrive by boat at ports such as Jaffa. Despite their poverty and lack of decent armour and weapons, they began to attract supporters from the West. Fulk V, Count of Anjou, met Hugues de Payen on his pilgrimage to Outremer in 1120, and was so impressed with Hugues and his nascent order that he enrolled as an associate of the Templars, pledging to give them an annual income of 30 *livres angevines*. Inspired by Fulk's example, several other French nobles did the same, perhaps the most important of them being Hugh, Count of Champagne.

Hugh had first visited Outremer in 1104, where he remained for four years. He returned again in 1114. On one of these occasions, he had been accompanied by Hugues de Payen. Hugues was one of his vassals, Payen being downriver from Troyes, where Hugh had his court. (In fact, Hugues may have even been related to his lord.) By the time Hugues and his eight companions took their vows in the Church of the Holy Sepulchre, Hugh had once again returned to France. He returned to the Holy Land for the last time in 1125, when he finally joined the Templars. But the full significance of Hugh's relationship to the Templars would have to wait another four years before becoming apparent.

In 1127, with the Templars still – according to the traditional story – only nine knights strong and struggling to recruit new members, King Baldwin II sent Hugues de

Payen and several other Templar brethren on a major diplomatic mission to Europe. That Hugues was chosen for such an important job suggests that, contrary to the stories of the Templars being 'poor knights', they were in fact by this time quite highly regarded in Outremer. In addition, Hugues took several knights with him, which, if they really were still only nine members strong, would have left only a few brethren back in Outremer. Indeed, chroniclers such as Michael the Syrian (d.1199), who was one of the first to document the Templars, believed that the Order had about 30 serving knights enlisted by the time of Baldwin's embassy.

The Templar delegation sailed to France, probably in the autumn of 1127, with William of Bures, the Prince of Galile, and Guy of Brisbarre, Lord of Beirut. William and Guy's mission was to persuade Fulk of Anjou to marry Baldwin's daughter, Melisende, and thereby stand to inherit the throne of Jerusalem, as Baldwin had no male heir. Whether Hugues' presence in the delegation was meant to persuade Fulk, who was one of the Templars' earliest supporters and donors, is not known, but even if it were, Hugues had been charged by Baldwin with another mission: to recruit knights for a projected crusade against Damascus, and to get the Templars officially recognised by the western Church.

The mission was a stunning success: Fulk agreed to return to Outremer and marry Melisende; many new recruits for Baldwin's Damascene Crusade were signed up; and, perhaps most importantly of all, Hugues met St Bernard of Clairvaux. It is from then on that, with St

Bernard's unwavering support, The Knights Templar emerged from the shadows on to the stage of European history in quite spectacular fashion.

The Council of Troyes

St Bernard of Clairvaux was the most influential Church Father of his time. A Burgundian noble, he was born at Fontaines-les-Dijons in 1090. While he was still in his mother's womb, a devout had predicted a great future for Bernard, and he seems to have grown into adulthood with a particular fervour and vision. Apparently a charismatic man of quite violent passions, he sought out a religious order whose austerity might help temper his volatile nature, and he entered the Cistercian order at Citeaux in 1113 with 30 or so fellow Burgundian nobles. Three years later, he led a small group of monks to found a new Cistercian house in the nearby valley of Wormwood, which they renamed Clairvaux, Valley of Light. Significantly, the land had been given to them by Hugh of Champagne, around the time of the Count's second pilgrimage to Outremer. The new foundation at Clairvaux under Bernard quickly became a magnet for the zealous, and the house flourished.

It is not known exactly when Bernard (he became a saint in 1174, a mere 21 years after his death) first became aware of the Templars or met Hugues de Payen. It is probable that King Baldwin wrote to Bernard in 1126 asking him to help devise a Rule for the Order, and to help win for them both recognition and support in the West.

Bernard was aware of the situation in the East, and realised that what Outremer needed were knights ready for active military service, not 'singing and wailing monks'.[5] Bernard's keen appreciation of the situation in Latin Syria most probably derived from his friendship with Hugh of Champagne, who had returned to the Holy Land for the third and final time in 1125, when he became a fully fledged Templar, and also from André de Montbard, who was not only one of the original nine knights, but was also Bernard's uncle. If Hugues and the Templar delegation did indeed sail to Europe during the autumn passage of 1127, then it is possible that Bernard met the Templar Grand Master towards the end of that year, or the following spring before Hugues started his mission proper, which would culminate with the Council of Troyes in January 1129.

As soon as Hugues arrived in Europe, things appeared to start moving very quickly. The Templars received their first grant of land in the West, with a house, a grange, a meadow and a tenement in Provins being given to the Order in October 1127, a gift from Hugh of Champagne's successor, Theobald, Count of Blois. Theobald also gave his vassals permission to donate freely to the Order from their own holdings of land. The Count of Flanders, William Clito, also donated to the Order around this time, as did his successor, Thierry of Alsace, after William's death in battle on 27 May 1128. Four days later, Hugues was in Anjou, where he witnessed Fulk take the Cross (a vow to defend Christianity from the infidel). On 17 June, he attended the wedding of Fulk's eldest son, Geoffrey, to Matilda, daughter of Henry I of England, which then left Fulk free to travel to Jerusalem as Baldwin had hoped. Further grants of land and money were made to Hugues, and it seems likely that the wedding led directly to Hugues being invited to England in the summer of 1128. Hugues' visit to England resulted in the establishment of the first Templar house, or preceptory, in London, at the north end of what is now Chancery Lane, in addition to gifts of money from the king and the acquisition of several sites outside of the capital. From England, Hugues travelled to Scotland before spending the autumn in Flanders, receiving further donations and preparing for Troyes.

When Hugues de Payen spoke before the Council of Troyes on 13 January 1129, he did so in front of an august assembly of churchmen. Not only was Bernard there in person (despite the fact that he was suffering from a fever), but also Stephen Harding, Abbott of Citeaux, the Archbishops of Sens and Rheims, ten bishops, Count Theobald of Champagne and, according to Jean Michel, the council's scribe, 'several others whom it would be tedious to record'. In addition to Hugues, the Templars were represented by Godfrey de St Omer, Geoffrey Bisol, Payen de Montdidier, Roland and Archambaud de St Aignan.[6] The whole delegation was presided over by the Papal Legate, Matthew of Albano.

In his speech, Hugues described the origins of the Order and the rule by which they lived: attending the offices; communal meals taken in silence; plain clothing; no women. Each brother swore vows of poverty, chastity and obedience upon entering the Order. As the brethren were frequently called out of the Temple on knightly business, they were each allowed one horse (although this was later increased to three), and a handful of servants. When away from the Temple, recitation of paternosters replaced hearing the offices. Knights and servants alike were under Hugues' command, with the whole order being answerable to the Patriarch of Jerusalem.

After some debate, the Council, under Bernard's supervision, drew up what became known as the Latin Rule of the Templars, which was based on the rule described by Hugues in his speech. It consisted of 73 clauses and regulated every aspect of Templar life. In addition to keeping the observances that the Order was already following, the Latin Rule advised the brethren how to admit newcomers to the Order, and how they should be vetted before being sworn in; at what age newcomers could join (boys being advised to wait until they were old enough to bear arms); how long brothers could serve for (which was usually a fixed term before allowing them to return to secular life if they so wished); how to reprimand miscreants and what offences would lead a brother to be expelled from the Order (such as deserting the battlefield, leaving a castle without permission or via an unauthorised exit), and so on. Knights were to wear white habits, to signify chastity and purity, while sergeants and squires were to wear brown or black (it must be remembered that the majority of Templars were not knights, but those who worked in the elaborate support network in the West that allowed them to remain on military duty in the East). The brethren's clothing and the bridles of their horses were to be unostentatious, avoiding such concessions to fashion as pointed shoes with laces and long hair. The Rule demanded short hair with a monk's tonsure; beards were mandatory.

There were two meals a day, around noon and then again at dusk, which were to be communal and silent, punctuated only by a reading from the scriptures. Meat was to be eaten only three times a week. No one was to get down from table unless there was a disturbance amongst the horses, or there was an impending attack. Physical relations with women were prohibited (although married men were admitted to the Order, provided they had their wives' consent). A yet more serious a crime was homosexuality, which was seen as being as bad as killing a fellow Christian. Idle talk was forbidden, with brethren expected to spend their free time maintaining the horses, equipment and clothing, or spending time in prayer.

Naturally, the Fathers gathered at Troyes had a great deal of clerical experience between them, but very little of campaigning in Outremer, so the Rule was more monastic than military, being principally concerned with the spiritual welfare of the Order's brethren. (It does make a few concessions to the actual physical conditions in the East, by allowing the brothers to wear linen shirts in the summer instead of the more customary European woollen equivalent.) Whatever shortcomings there were in the original 1129 Rule, they would later be rectified in the 1160s, and then again in the 1260s. By the time of the Order's downfall, the Rule had grown to contain 686 clauses.

Daily life in a Templar preceptory was much the same as that of a Western monastery. The day would begin (during the summer months) with matins at 4:00am, which comprised the saying of 13 paternosters. The brothers were then permitted a brief sleep until the division bell summoned them to prime at 6:00am, when the first mass of the day was said. Terce was at 8:00am, and sext at 11:30am, which was followed by the first meal of the day. Usually the knights ate first, followed by the sergeants. Nones was at 2:00pm, followed by vespers at 6:00pm. The evening meal would then be taken, with the final office of the day, compline, being said around 8:00pm. As the winter months brought shorter daylight hours, the offices would be compressed so that matins would always begin after first light, and compline would similarly occur around the onset of twilight.

'A Certain New Monster'

When Hugues de Payen returned to Outremer after the Council of Troyes, he did so as the head of an order which was now in a greatly enhanced position. Nevertheless, the Templars were not universally welcomed by all quarters of the Church. During the tenth and eleventh centuries, the Church had gone through a great wave of reforms championed by Pope Gregory VII (1073–85), which had led to the establishment of such houses as Cluny and Citeaux. The reformers of Bernard's generation and the generation before stressed spiritual purity untainted by politics and especially bloodshed. They strove to maintain a distance between temporal monarchy and spiritual matters. Henry of Huntingdon was to describe the mix of monk and soldier as 'a certain new monster,' while Guigo, the prior of La Grande Chartreuse, wrote to Hugues to warn of the dangers of mixing the military and the monastic:

> 'It is useless indeed for us to attack exterior enemies if we do not first conquer those of the interior ... Let us first purge our souls of vices, then the lands from the barbarians.'[7]

Guigo implored Hugues to read the letter to all the brethren and even went so far as to send the letter twice via different couriers to ensure that at least one copy reached its destination.

A letter exists from around this time that is addressed to Templar brethren, which was authored by a 'Hugues,' although this has never been proven to be by Hugues de Payen. The writer has simply signed himself as '*Hugo peccator*' – Hugh the Sinner – and it is conceivable that it is the work of the theologian Hugh of St Victor. Regardless of authorship, the letter is ample evidence that external criticism of the Order had filtered through the ranks. It begins ' ... we have heard that certain of you have been troubled by persons of little wisdom',[8] and proceeds to warn the brethren of the Devil and all his works. Hugo stresses the need for the brothers to be mindful of their inner state, and to accept their lot, reminding them that their personal salvation has to be worked for.

Whether or not Hugues de Payen wrote the '*Hugo peccator*' letter, he seems at the very least to have been aware of it, as he asked Bernard of Clairvaux no fewer than three times to compose a defence of the Order, as if to settle the matter once and for all. Bernard, by now the Order's most prominent supporter, did not disappoint. The treatise he wrote, *In Praise of the New Knighthood*, draws a distinction between the old, secular knighthood that had predominated since the days of Charlemagne, and the new, monastic knighthood as personified by the Templars. By doing so, Bernard was going against the drift of Gregory VII's reforms. He went even further by arguing that knighthood was compatible with monasticism: the knights' duty was to kill for Christ and, in doing so, would rid the world of evil, not evil-doers. He argued that there was a difference between *homicide* – killing, which was a sin – and *malecide* – the killing of evil, which was not. Not only was it possible to gain Christ by dying for him, it was, according to Bernard, also possible to attain salvation by killing for him as well. A more concise argument in favour of holy war would be difficult to imagine.

Whatever criticisms the Order faced immediately after the triumph of Troyes, they did not seem to impede the willingness of nobles to help in the fight against the infidel. Baldwin's attack on Damascus in November 1129 comprised a number of Templars in addition to a great number of men whom Hugues had recruited during the European tour. The expedition got within six miles of Damascus before a breakaway contingent under William of Bures decided that the time was ripe for some pillaging. William lost control of the group, and they were attacked by Damascene cavalry. There were only 45 survivors. Baldwin hoped to catch the Damascenes off guard as they were celebrating their victory over the Franks, but as Baldwin's troops readied for an attack, the rains came down, making the roads so impassable that the offensive had to be called off.

The failure of the attack on Damascus did not seem to affect the Templars adversely. Donations, which throughout the Order's existence usually came in the form of grants of land and buildings (together with the people who lived there) and the right to receive the revenues from them, not only continued, but accelerated. Usually, the reasons for donations were to confirm the donor's piety, in the same way that rich merchants or worthies might commission the building of a chapel that would help exonerate their sins and stand them in good stead in the next world. The fight against the infidel was seen in the same terms, and the Templars found no shortage of penitents who wished to wipe their slates clean.

The most extensive donation came in October 1131, when the Templars – together with the other main military order, the Knights Hospitaller and the Church of the Holy Sepulchre in Jerusalem – were left the entire Kingdom of Aragon in the will of its ruler, Alfonso I, 'The Battler'. Aragon under Alfonso had expanded rapidly since 1118, and the gains had been so great that Alfonso's resources were becoming increasingly stretched. The Iberian peninsula had been invaded by Muslim forces in 711, but the Christian counterattack, known as the *Reconquista*, began almost at once. When an alliance of Visigoths and Asturians defeated a Muslim army at Covadonga in 722, none of them could have known that the process of reclaiming the peninsula for Christ would take centuries of conflict.

Alfonso's response to maintaining his newly enlarged lands was to establish confraternities of knights to guard against any further Muslim reconquest, and the orders he established between 1122 and 1130, such as the orders of Belchite and Monreal del Campo, were similar to the Templars in that brothers served for a set time, but were not required to take monastic vows. The project was not entirely successful, however, as the Order of Monreal del Campo was on the verge of fizzling out by the time Alfonso drew up his will, with the result that the military orders of the East seemed to be the best solution to the problem. In addition, Alfonso was childless, which made securing the kingdom even more of a priority. Although Alfonso died in 1134, it took nine years for the will to be enforced, so enormous were the complexities of bequeathing such vast areas of land to so few beneficiaries. Although the Templars inherited somewhat less than Alfonso originally intended, they nonetheless were left with huge tracts of land across his former kingdom. From then on, the Templars would almost totally replace Alfonso's stillborn orders and become a major force in the *Reconquista* against the forces of Islam.

Shortly after Alfonso's death, the Templars began to receive castles in Outremer. The first were not in the Kingdom of Jerusalem at all, but north of Antioch in what was known as the Amanus March. This was a mountainous region that connected the Principality of Antioch with Cilician Armenia, and the Templars were given the task of guarding the Belen Pass. The first fortress they were given was Baghras, which they renamed Gaston, followed by

Darbsaq, la Roche de Roussel and Roche Guillame. To the south-west of these strongholds was Port Bonnel, given to the Order at around the same time, which gave them access to the sea. In frontier regions such as the Amanus March, Templar properties such as Barghas were always fortified as they were places of high strategic value. Given the ever unstable situation in the East, almost all Templar properties had some kind of fortification, whether they were castles or not. In the West, on the other hand, most Templar preceptories were not fortified, as they were not situated in potentially hostile areas (the exceptions being on the Iberian peninsula, where the threat of Moorish aggression was never far away, and also in eastern Europe, where the military orders campaigned against the indigenous pagans).

If the ever-increasing flow of money and property into the Temple's coffers was helping to alleviate doubts – both within and without the Order – about the purpose, effectiveness and morality of the Templars, then the three papal bulls (named after the *bullum*, or seal, used on the parchment) secured by Robert de Craon, the second Grand Master, raised the Order above any official reproach save that from the Papacy itself. It did not put an end to commentators criticising the Templars, but the bulls put them in a position where such comments were superfluous. Put simply, from 1139, just as they were establishing themselves in the Amanus March, the Templars, on something of a roll since the Council of Troyes, became untouchable.

Papal Approval: The Three Bulls

Robert de Craon, known as 'Robert the Burgundian', despite the fact that he was a native of Anjou, succeeded Hugues de Payen as Grand Master after the latter's death (which occurred on 24 May, probably in 1136). He was a skilful administrator, and knew that if the Order was ever to consolidate the gains made at Troyes, then nothing less than Papal privileges would secure them. Three years later, that is exactly what he secured from Pope Innocent II.

The bull *Omne datum optimum*, drawn up at the Lateran on 29 March 1139, made the Templars answerable to none save the Pontiff himself. The bull confirmed the Rule of the Order, and also all donations made to it. In addition, the workings of the Order were addressed: the Templars were allowed to elect their own Master without outside interference; only the Master could change the Order's customs and observances, although only after consulting the Chapter of Brothers (the Chapter was a sort of ruling council of each preceptory); the brothers were forbidden to give oaths of loyalty to anyone outside of the Order; and no professed brother was allowed to return to the secular world or join another order. The bull went on to exempt the Templars from paying tithes, but allowed them to receive them from clergy and laity alike, provided that the tithes were presented as gifts freely given (a privilege that had previously only applied to the Cistercians).

Aside from allowing the Order to keep all booty captured from the Muslims, the remainder of the bull was concerned with the Order's spiritual life. The Templars could receive clerks and priests to serve the Order, but first needed the consent of the priest's bishop. If the bishop refused, he could be overruled by the Pope himself. The Order retained the right to remove a priest if he caused disturbances within the Order or proved himself to be more of a hindrance than an asset, provided that the Chapter approved. However, a priest might be allowed to join the Order after he had served for one year, if the brothers approved. The priests would not be called upon to fight, but to have care of the brothers' souls only. The priests would not be subject to anyone from outside the Order, and the Templars had the right to have their clergy ordained by any bishop. Furthermore, the Order's clergy were not allowed to preach for money, unless by prior arrangement with the Master. The Templars were to be allowed to build oratories on their land, and be permitted to hear divine office there. Serving brothers could be buried there when they died. Wherever they travelled, the brothers could hear confession from any priest, and receive any sacrament or unction. The privileges set out in *Omne datum optimum* also covered the Templars' household and servants. The bull ended with Innocent quoting 1 Corinthians, Chapter 7, Verse 20: 'each of you to remain in that vocation to which you are called'.

The privileges granted to the Templars by Innocent were reinforced by his successors, Celestine II and Eugenius III. *Milites Templi*, issued by Celestine in 1144, was addressed to the clergy. In this, the Templars were described as defending pilgrims and protecting the Church from the pagans; as a result, the clergy were ordered to make a collection for the Templars. Celestine urged donors to form confraternities to support the Order, and whosoever joined one would have one-seventh of his penance remitted. As a further perk, members of the confraternities would have the right to be buried in churches unless they had been excommunicated. When the Templars came to collect the confraternity's money, the churches would be opened on one day a year for that purpose only, and the offices heard. *Militia Dei*, issued the following year, was again addressed to the clergy, and gave the Templars further privileges. Eugenius promised not to damage their rights, and announced that the Templars had permission to take on priests for their Order. The priests needed to be properly ordained and have their bishop's permission before they could serve the Order. The brothers could take tithes and burial offerings where they had a house, and could build oratories and bury their brothers and servants when they died. Eugenius asked the clergy to consecrate Templar oratories, bless their cemeteries and allow their priests to work in peace.

The three bulls legitimised the Templars and firmly established them at the heart of Christendom's efforts in the Holy Land. Although criticism of the Order was to continue, there was little any critic could do; the Templars were above reproach. It had been a remarkable ascendancy – from the Council of Troyes, the Templars had gone from being a slightly shady organisation of unknown provenance to being the defenders of the one true faith in a mere 15 years. For the next century and a half, their position would remain unassailable; few could have predicted that their eventual fall would be as meteorically swift as their rise.

A Church within a Church,
a State within a State
(1145–1291)

The Second Crusade

The Second Crusade (1147–49) provided a measure of how successfully the Templars had established themselves in the years after the Council of Troyes and the three great bulls of privilege. On Christmas Eve 1144, the city of Edessa fell to an army under the command of Imad ad-Din Zengi, the *Atabeg* (governor) of Mosul and Aleppo. When news finally reached Pope Eugenius III the following autumn, he immediately wrote to King Louis VII of France, imploring him to lead a new crusade to rescue Edessa from the infidel. Louis was not at all popular in France at the time, as three years earlier he had started a war when he illegally seized lands belonging to his most powerful vassal, Theobald of Champagne, and he seems to have been surprised when none of his barons showed much interest in his proposal for a new expedition to the East. It was decided that the matter would be settled at a meeting at Vézelay in Burgundy at Easter 1146. Realising that he was potentially without allies, Louis turned to the one man who had the clout to rally would-be crusaders, and that was Bernard of Clairvaux.

The scene at Vézelay on 31 March 1146 was reminiscent of Clermont in 1095 – huge crowds had gathered, drawn by the prospect of hearing Bernard preach the crusade. So many had arrived in Vézelay that Bernard had to deliver his sermon from a specially constructed platform on the outskirts of town. Bernard's words found a receptive audience. As soon as he had finished speaking, King Louis was the first to pledge allegiance, followed by his brother Robert, the Count of Dreux. Of all of those who vowed to journey to the East that day, many were the sons and grandsons of the original crusaders, to whom maintaining family honour was at least as important as liberating Edessa. Bernard later wrote to King Louis of the success of Vézelay: 'Villages and towns are now deserted ... Everywhere you will see widows whose husbands are still alive.'[9]

On 27 April 1147, a Chapter meeting of the Paris Temple welcomed both King Louis and Pope Eugenius in the build-up to the crusade's departure. Also present were four archbishops, 130 Templar knights and at least as many Templar sergeants and squires. Eugenius appointed Aymar, the Templar treasurer, to receive the tax that he had imposed on all Church goods to finance the crusade. William of Tyre, the great chronicler who was writing a generation later, believed that it was at this meeting that the Pope conferred on the Templars the right to wear a red cross on their white mantles, which symbolised their willingness to suffer martyrdom in defending the Holy Land against the infidel.

Germany was fermenting with crusading zeal by this

time, after King Conrad III had heard Bernard preach in the Rhineland. Eugenius had originally wanted Conrad to help in the fight against his primary foe, the Norman king, Roger of Sicily, but as Conrad could not be dissuaded from going on crusade, it was decided that he should lead a German force that would work alongside the French.

Everard des Barres, Master of the Temple in France, together with the knights present at the April Chapter meeting, accompanied the French army under Louis on the overland route taken by the First Crusade. Everard proved himself to be one of Louis' most trusted advisors, and the French king sent the Templar Master ahead to Constantinople to negotiate the Crusade's passage through Byzantine territory. Unlike his predecessor Alexius, the Byzantine Emperor Manuel Comnenus had not asked for Western help, and was somewhat nervous at the prospect of the crusading force (made up largely of the French and German armies) bearing down upon his lands. Everard succeeded in getting the Crusaders through, although Manuel was looked upon with grave suspicion by the Franks, as he had signed a peace treaty with the Seljuk Turks in order to wage war against Roger of Sicily. Manuel was equally uneasy with the crusaders, and was glad to see the back of them.

In January 1148, the Crusade got into further difficulty. Demoralised by severe weather and the news that Conrad's army – which had gone ahead of the French – had suffered a defeat at Dorylaeum by the Seljuk Turks, the French came under attack in the narrow passes of the Cadmus mountains. The Franks' heavy cavalry was useless in such terrain, and the columns of crusaders came under constant attack from the Turkish light infantry, whose archers were masters of firing from the saddle. The Franks were further hampered by an acute shortage of horses and provisions, and it seemed as though the Crusade would be over before it ever reached Outremer. Once again, Louis turned to Everard des Barres and the Templars. Everard broke the army up into units of 50, each under the command of a Templar, who in turn were answerable to another Templar knight, Brother Gilbert. This provided the beleaguered French with sufficient morale and order to continue as far as the Byzantine port of Attalia, where Louis took his best troops by boat to Antioch.

At Antioch, the Crusade took yet another turn for the worse. Louis had all but exhausted his funds in getting the army across Asia Minor; once again, Everard des Barres was the man to whom Louis turned for help. On 10 May, Everard sailed from Antioch to Acre, where he raised sufficient capital to fund the rest of the crusade, either by drawing directly from the treasury at the Templar preceptory in Acre, or by borrowing using the Order's possessions as security. Whichever was the case, it proved that the Templars had become a major financial institution, and it cemented the relationship between the Order and the French crown, with the result that the Templars effectively became the French royal treasury until the late thirteenth century.

The Templars seem to have played a less prominent role in the remainder of the crusade. A council of war was convened at Acre in June to decide on a course of action, with the Templar Grand Master Robert de Craon present, together with the Grand Master of the Hospital, Raymond du Puy. After debating whether they should head for Edessa via Aleppo, or whether they should instead strike out for Ascalon in the south, it was eventually decided that the target should be Damascus, which the crusaders planned to attack the following month. After initial success in besieging the city from the west, the crusaders made the tactical blunder of decamping to a position on the east of the city. Unlike their original position, which had been well supplied, this new eastern position had no water and also faced the best fortified section of the city walls. With rumours that a huge Muslim army under Zengi's son Nur ed-Din (Zengi having died in 1146) was on its way, the crusaders lost their nerve and retreated. The Second Crusade was over, and the recriminations for its failure began.

There were various theories as to why the Second Crusade had been such a fiasco. Accusations of treachery abounded, with various parties being named as the chief culprits. The crusaders, unused to life in the East, were shocked by the way Christians in Outremer had assimilated Eastern ways, and the 'Men of Jerusalem', as they were called, were seen as the guilty party by a number of commentators in the West. John of Würzburg, a German monk who travelled to Outremer in the 1160s, believed that the Crusade's failure was due to Templar treachery. John's anonymous colleague, known as the Würzburg Annalist, went even further, and stated that the Templars had been paid off by the Damascenes to lift the siege. Only later was it found that the money the Orders had been paid was in fact counterfeit, which was seen as Divine punishment for betraying the Christian cause. Other variants of the story had the 'Men of Jerusalem' accepting the money, while the early thirteenth-century chronicle of Ernoul and Bernard the Treasurer had the Hospitallers working alongside the Templars in putting profit before God. However, the Military Orders' sternest critic of the time, William of Tyre, does not mention either the Templars or the Hospitallers in connection with the failure of the Crusade. As the bad press the orders received dates from several decades later, it would seem that the chroniclers were reflecting contemporary disillusion with both the Temple and the Hospital and projecting it back to 1148.

Given that the Templars played a major role in financing the Second Crusade, it might be worth examining the role the Order played in the financial affairs of both Outremer and the West, and the subsequent dominance they exerted over what was to evolve into a system of international banking.

The Temple as Bankers

The Templars quite early on in their history developed a reputation for being reliable bankers. They were – in effect – Europe's first bank. They developed a system of credit notes whereby money deposited in one Templar preceptory could be withdrawn at another upon production of a credit note. Monies thus deposited proved to be quite safe, as Templar keeps were formidable buildings. Some of their castles in Outremer, for instance, were so well defended that they were impregnable (such as their massive fortress at 'Atlīt, which was actually a fortified peninsula rather than a mere castle). In Europe, the imposing edifice of the Paris Temple became their financial base (as did, to a lesser extent, the London Temple).

Louis VII was the first of a number of European monarchs whose finances were saved from collapse by Templar loans, although the size of the loan that the Templars provided brought the Order close to bankruptcy. It is thought that the Order provided him with 2,000 marks of silver and 30,000 *livres parisis*. The magnitude of this amount of money can be seen when it is compared to revenues from French royal lands which, even 20 or so years after the Second Crusade, were only about 60,000 *livres parisis* per year.

Louis VII was not the only French monarch who was to become reliant on the Order's financial services. The Second Crusade saw the beginning of a long association between the Order and the kings of France. By the reign of Philip II (1180–1223), the Templars were effectively the French royal treasury. During the course of his reign, they increased the revenues from royal estates by 120 per cent, and were heavily involved in Philip's restructuring of Capetian finances. During the thirteenth century, the Templar treasurer in Paris was always a man selected by the king, and the treasurers became trusted advisers to Philip and his successors. When Louis' great-grandson, Louis IX, was held hostage after the disasters of the Seventh Crusade in 1250, it was to the Temple that the French commanders looked for the remaining 30,000 *livres* that they required to bail him out (although, on this occasion the Templar commander, Stephen of Otricourt, was less than happy to comply).

That the Templars proved themselves to be so successful as bankers is due in no large part to the meticulousness of their records, and their objectivity in dealing with clients. Records survive from the Paris Temple for the period 12 March 1295 to 4 July the following year, and they give a clear indication of how busy the Paris Temple was in its role as banker. These records – eight surviving sheets of parchment – record the date and the Templar on duty at the time, in addition to the amount deposited, by whom, into which account the money should be paid and from where the amount came from. At the end of each day, the receipts collected would be taken to the strong rooms to be deposited. (During the 1260s and 1270s, a great tower was built in order to house the various monies the Order was keeping.) There were more than 60 active accounts at the Paris Temple during this period, with the account holders being a mixture of royalty, clergy, important nobles and Templar officials. No business was done at Christmas, Easter and Ascension, and also on the Feast Days of saints who had a particular relevance for the Order, such as John the Baptist. Outside of these dates, the hours the Temple was open for business depended largely on the needs of its clients. In August 1295, for instance, they were only open for six days, whereas that December, they were far busier, being at one point open on 11 consecutive days. The Paris Temple also sent out statements to important clients several times a year, detailing the movements within their accounts.

Matters did not always go smoothly, however, as the chronicler Joinville discovered to his cost on the Seventh Crusade. While the army was recuperating at Acre following King Louis' ransom, Joinville received 400 *livres* in wages. He kept 40 and deposited the remaining 360 with the Templars. When he sent one of his men to withdraw another 40 for current living expenses, the Templar treasurer denied all knowledge of Joinville and his savings. Joinville then complained to the newly elected Grand Master, Reginald de Vichiers, who was initially dubious at Joinville's accusation that the treasurer had lost his money. Reginald looked into the matter, and several days later was able to report to a much relieved Joinville that his money had been found; the treasurer was transferred out of Acre.

The Papacy also came to be dependent on the Templars for its financial needs. The Templars were acting as Pope Alexander III's (1159–81) bankers from as early as 1163, and, as they had been involved with the overhaul of Capetian finances under Philip II, so the Order was also used by Pope Innocent III when he undertook to reorganise crusading finances at the time of the Fourth Crusade (1202–4). A new tax, levied on the clergy for the express purpose of being used to fund the campaigns in the East, was to be paid into Templar and Hospitaller preceptories; the military orders would then be responsible for transporting the money safely to the Holy Land. A similar procedure was followed by Honorius III when he was raising funds for the Fifth Crusade (1218–21), with the money raised to be transferred to the papal legate in Egypt.

Kings from other countries likewise came to the

Temple. The kings of Aragon were heavy borrowers, and King Henry II of England (1154–89) used the Order to accumulate crusading funds in Jerusalem, whilst his brother King John (1199–1216) was borrowing anything from nine marks of gold for an offering to be made when he was absolved following the lifting of his excommunication in 1213, to loans of over 4,000 marks two years later to pay the wages of troops in Poitou and Gascony. During his wars with the barons, John's son Henry III (1216–72) moved the crown jewels to the Paris Temple for safekeeping in 1261, where they were inventoried and stored until further notice. The further notice duly came three years later, when Henry used them as security on a loan to finance further campaigns against the barons.

The Templars' financial services were not restricted to providing loans, however, and not just for the royalty and nobility. As crusaders and pilgrims might be away from Europe for several years, the Templars also accepted precious documents and objects for safekeeping, including wills. One such example was the will of Pierre Sarrasin, which was drawn up in June 1220 before he set out for Santiago de Compostella. In it, he specified that, if he failed to return, the Templars should pay 600 *livres parisis* to the Abbey of St Victor, and that this should be used to buy rents from corn, the annual proceeds from which (about 200 *livres parisis*) were to be used to make daily donations of bread; furthermore, there were additional beneficiaries, including his mother, who was to be paid 100 *livres*. The remainder of the estate was to be held by the Templars until Pierre's heirs came of age.

The Structure of the Order

As the Temple grew from being the original nine soldier-monks sworn to poverty, chastity and obedience into what we would nowadays recognise as a multinational corporation, so too did the structure of the Order evolve to reflect and support its expanding role in the affairs of the crusader states.

The Grand Master was the absolute ruler over the Order; after the bull *Omne datum optimum* of 1139 he was answerable only to the Pope. Grand Masters were chosen by an electoral college of 13 senior Templars, comprising eight knights, four sergeants and one chaplain. Generally, the electoral college would try to choose someone who was already based in the East. Given the importance of the Paris Temple to the French monarchy, French kings could – and often did – influence the choice of a Grand Master, such as during the election of Reginald de Vichiers in 1250. As the Order expanded, so did the trappings of office: by the time of Bertrand de Blancfort's tenure (1156–69), a Grand Master could expect to have four horses, and an entourage made up of two knights, a sergeant, a chaplain, a turcopolier, a farrier, a cook and a Saracen secretary. The Master also had first choice whenever the Order received a fresh batch of horses from the West.

Immediately beneath the Grand Master was a Chapter of senior officials. The Seneschal was both deputy and adviser to the Grand Master. On occasion, Seneschals would eventually become 'promoted' to Grand Master – the politics of the electoral college permitting – such as André de

Montbard, who was one of Hugues de Payen's original knights. After acting as Seneschal for four years, he finally became Grand Master in 1153 after the short Mastership of Bernard de Tremelay had come to an abrupt and bloody end at Ascalon. Like the Grand Master, the Seneschal also had his own staff. The Marshal was responsible for all military decisions, such as the purchase of horses and equipment, and also had jurisdiction over the regional commanders. These were commanders who had responsibility for one specific area: the Commander of the Kingdom of Jerusalem acted as the Order's treasurer, oversaw the Kingdom and had the same powers as the Grand Master within it; the Commander of the City of Jerusalem, who likewise was overlord of the city only, also had the same powers as the Grand Master within its walls; and the commanders of Tripoli, Acre and Antioch were invested with similar powers. Each major kingdom in the West with a significant Templar presence had a Master who was answerable to the Grand Master: France, England, Aragon, Portugal, Poitou, Apulia and Hungary. The Draper was responsible for the issue of clothing and bedding, and made sure that individual brothers did not hoard private property. He was also authorised to distribute gifts made to the Order.

There were further roles that seem to have been subservient to the various masters and commanders. The Commander of Houses was responsible for specific Templar houses in the East and was answerable to the higher ranks; the Commander of Knights acted as deputy to the Commander of the Kingdom of Jerusalem; the

Turcopolier, who was in charge of the turcopoles (the light cavalry who were often local troops engaged for a fixed period); the Under Marshal, who oversaw the footmen and the equipment; the Standard Bearer, who was usually a sergeant and was responsible for the conduct of the squires; and the Infirmarer looked after sick and aged brothers, who would often be sent back to reside in the Order's Western houses, away from the front lines of Outremer and the Iberian Peninsula.

The elite of the Templar fighting force was comprised of the group perhaps most readily pictured when we think of the Order – the knights with their white mantles bearing the distinctive red cross over the heart. They would already be expected to be skilled in the arts of war before joining the Order, when they would hand over their secular clothes and be issued with armour, equipment and clothing to wear when not in the field. Although originally knights could be from any social group (including excommunicates, such was the constant need for manpower in the East), by the time of the Second Crusade it was necessary for knights to be descended from knightly stock. Each knight would be granted three horses and a squire, whose role would be to assist the knight and to make sure that he was fully equipped and ready to go into battle. Like the turcopoles, squires were usually not fully sworn-in Templars, but often locals who were hired for a set period.

The other main group of fighting Templars was the sergeants, who, unlike the knights, wore black or brown mantles, and were not as heavily armed. Sergeants were from a much more socially and racially mixed background than the knights, and their ranks were often made up with men of Armenian and Syrian origin. They had to make do with only one horse, and were required to be their own squires.

Gaza and Ascalon

Despite the major setback of the Second Crusade, the Christian presence in Outremer continued to be pre-emptive. The one coastal city that remained in Muslim hands was Ascalon, and a series of forts had been built around it to hem it in. During the winter of 1149–50, King Baldwin III gave the Templars Gaza, which lay a dozen or so miles to the south. The city was largely in ruins, and the Templars set about rebuilding the fort – it was the first important castle the Order received in the Kingdom of Jerusalem. The Egyptian forces, now unable to supply Ascalon by land, tried to retake Gaza almost as soon as the Templars had acquired the city; the attempt failed.

The siege of Ascalon finally began on 25 January 1153, and the campaign reached its climax during the summer. On the night of 15 August, a sortie of defenders from the city set fire to the Franks' mobile siege tower. The wind changed direction, however, and blew the flames back against the city walls. The ensuing fire caused part of the wall to collapse, and a Templar contingent under the Grand Master, Bernard de Tremelay, rushed into the breach. The chronicler William of Tyre records that Bernard forbade non-Templars to enter the city, such was the Templar greed for booty. They made an unsuccessful stand in the city; the next day, their beheaded bodies were hung over the walls of Ascalon. No Muslim source records this incident, and it is possible that William was venting his habitual ire; rather than a desire for booty, Bernard and his men may have simply perished trying to hold open the breach in the wall. Either way, the city fell a week later, and the Templars' reputation for avarice had begun.

The Templars in the West

What had seemed, to commentators in both Outremer and the West, to be an avaricious streak in the Order of the Temple was, in many cases, merely a misunderstanding of the fact that the Order ran its estates with scrupulous care. The land donated to them in the West since Hugues de Payen's visit of 1127–29 formed the basis of the Order's wealth. As Malcolm Barber has noted, 'without an extensive network of support in the West, the Templars would have vanished with the first major defeat they suffered'.[10] This network took the form of their European preceptories, which were initially acquired through the extensive programme of donations that transpired during and after Hugues de Payen's tour.

Ordinarily, a Templar preceptory would be an estate (a farm or a manor, for instance) that would then develop a network of daughter houses around it. All the revenues from both the mother and daughter houses would be directed towards campaigning in the East. A tax, known as the *responsion*, was raised, whereby one-third of all revenues collected from a Templar house in the West was to be used to support the Order's work in the Holy Land. These

Western houses were generally established in all the main cities, financial centres and ports of Europe. Wherever there was trade, there were Templars.

The preceptories not only kept the Order bankrolled, but also supplied food, clothes, arms and horses. This, together with the Templars' increasingly important role in the East, meant that the work of the Western houses was even more vital in keeping the Order freshly supplied. With rising prices in the thirteenth century, the onus was on the preceptories to maintain a permanent vigilance over their accounts, and to be constantly on the look-out for new ways to make money. Thus, the Order's holdings expanded to include not just farmland, but also wine presses, orchards and even tile factories. To gain further support, the Templars introduced a kind of affiliate membership whereby one could, after a donation, hear Mass in a Templar church and have the right to burial in a Templar cemetery. In some cases, the Templars provided these donors with a pension if there was no one else to look after them.

The majority of the Templars' 9,000 Western manors were in France, and, to a lesser extent, Italy. While the Order had property in Germany, that country was largely the province of the Teutonic Knights. Likewise, on the Iberian Peninsula, the Templars – although heavily involved in the *Reconquista* – generally had a lower profile than that of the great Spanish and Portuguese orders, Calatrava, Santiago and Alcántara. In England, the Order's base was at the London Temple, with its holdings being scattered across the country, from Penzance and the island of Lundy in the Bristol Channel to Yorkshire and Lincolnshire. Generally speaking, any modern English place name that has the prefix of 'Temple' was once owned by the Order.

The Temple and the Crescent Moon

One of the reasons why the Second Crusade was seen to have failed was perfidy on the part of the 'Men of Jerusalem' and the Military Orders. The Crusaders under Louis VII had been shocked at how much the Latins in Outremer had adopted Eastern ways, unaware that in many cases the adoption of local custom was the most pragmatic thing to do. The culture of the Arab world was more refined than the culture most Crusaders had known in the West:

> 'The Franks employed Syrian doctors, cooks, servants, artisans, labourers. They clothed themselves in Eastern garments, included in their diets the fruits and dishes of the country. They had glass in their windows, mosaics on their floors, fountains in the courtyards of their houses, which were planned on the Syrian model. They had dancing girls at their entertainments; professional mourners at their funerals; took baths; used soap; ate sugar.'[11]

In addition, the Franks in Outremer had fresh produce all year round, including fruit and vegetables that were unknown in Europe, such as peaches, olives and bananas.

There were more serious practicalities, however.

Although Jerusalem was in Christian hands, the majority of the population remained Muslim. Although they remained second-class citizens unless they converted, they were allowed to choose their own community leaders and, as long as they paid their taxes on time, their Christian rulers were content to let them be. Similarly, the Jewish community remained relatively unharassed (which was in remarkable contrast to the atrocities committed against both communities during the First Crusade).

The Templars showed a great deal of tolerance towards Islam. As has been noted, Grand Masters always had Saracen secretaries, and it was not uncommon for Templars to learn Arabic. One Muslim ambassador visiting the Templars in Jerusalem was given a small chapel in which to pray; when a Frank tried to stop him, the Templars dragged the man off and let the ambassador say his prayers to Mecca in peace.

One group with whom the Templars had a less convivial relationship was the Assassins. They were a fanatical sect of Shi'ite Muslims, who had broken away in the late eleventh century from the Fatimids, the main Shi'ite regime, and set themselves up in the Elburz mountains in northern Persia and later in the mountains of the Lebanon; their leader became known to the Franks as 'the Old Man of the Mountains'. The Shi'ites were strongly messianic and mystical, believing in the coming of the Mahdi, 'the Guided One', who would appear to destroy tyranny and establish Paradise. They pursued their goals through an unpredictable campaign of terror in which Assassin killers would murder their opponents in audacious – sometimes suicidal

– attacks. (Their name derives from *hashishim*, an ingester of hashish. The drug was said to make the taker oblivious to danger.) Frequently, these victims were Muslims from the main rival sect of Islam, the Sunnis, or even other Shi'ite groups.

In 1173, the King of Jerusalem, Amalric I (1162–74), attempted to negotiate an alliance with the Assassins, as Amalric was given to believe that the Old Man of the Mountains was about to convert to Christianity. This was perhaps not as ludicrous as it may sound, as the Old Man had, just a few years earlier, abrogated the law of the Prophet and proclaimed the Millennium, thus making himself and the rest of the sect heretical. The Templars were less certain about the Old Man's threatened apostasy, and a group of Templar knights ambushed Abdullah, the Old Man's envoy, near Tripoli and killed him. Amalric was furious, and commentators such as William of Tyre and Walter Map seized upon the opportunity to launch another attack on the greed of the Temple: in their view, the Order was afraid of losing its annual tribute of 2,000 *besants* that the Assassins paid to the Templars to leave them largely alone. The Grand Master, Odo de St Amand, refused to hand over the killer, a one-eyed knight by the name of Walter of Mesnil, saying that Innocent's great bull of 1139 put the Templars above the jurisdiction of the throne of Jerusalem, and he would instead send Walter to Rome to be dealt with. Amalric ignored this and seized Walter at Sidon, where the Templar chapter was in session, and had him cast into prison. Amalric managed to persuade the Old Man that the Templars had been acting on their own, but all attempts at forging an alliance with the Assassins were dropped.

The incident showed that, if need be, the Templars would not only go against a Muslim group who, if not actual allies, were at least tolerated and accorded some degree of respect, but also the King of Jerusalem himself. A reason for the murder has never been fully established. That the Templars were afraid of losing their tribute is unlikely, given the wealth of the Order by this time; perhaps they knew only too well that the Assassins could not be entirely trusted, and a breakaway Templar faction under Walter of Mesnil decided to take matters into its own hands.

The Temple as Architects

The Affair of the Assassin Envoy, as it came to be known, shows how far the Order had become independent of all authority save that of the Pope himself, and detractors, railing against the privileges that the Templars enjoyed, accused them of having become 'a church within a church, a state within a state'. Such criticism appeared to have no effect on the Order, however, and, if the Templars' building programme in the East is any indicator, it probably only reinforced their belief that they were different because it was the will of God.

Templar masons built a number of churches throughout Latin Syria, and were involved in several major projects, including the construction of the new Church of the Holy Sepulchre, dedicated in 1149, and the renovation of the

Church of the Nativity in Bethlehem. In addition, they provided an elaborate tomb for Baldwin IV, the leper king, upon his death in 1185. Their churches and buildings in the West tended to be simpler, with major expense being reserved for important preceptories such as Paris and London. Likewise, not all their churches boasted the distinctive round design, such as the Temple Church in London. (The round churches were apparently inspired by the Temple of the Lord in Jerusalem.) Regional preceptories, such as Temple Garway in Herefordshire, were simple, austere but functional places.

The other major feat of Templar architecture in the East was the fortresses they either reinforced, rebuilt or had constructed especially for them. Castles such as Safad in Galilee, Tortosa in the County of Tripoli and 'Atlīt on the coast south of Haifa were masterpieces of medieval military architecture. Indeed, so strong were the fortifications at 'Atlīt – its outer walls were 15ft (4.5m) thick – that it even managed to withstand a major assault while it was still being built.

The Templars had, in fact, been closely involved with building projects since their inception. When King Baldwin II had moved out of the al-Aqsa mosque during the 1120s, the Templars were given free reign to develop the area as they saw fit. Theoderich, a German monk who visited the Holy Land between 1169 and 1174, wrote a detailed account of the Temple area:

'One follows to the south [from the Dome of the Rock, rechristened the Temple of the Lord after the First

Crusade], and there is the Palace of Solomon [al-Aqsa]. Like a church it is oblong and supported by pillars, and also at the end of the sanctuary it rises up to a circular roof, large and round, and also like a church. This and all its neighbouring buildings have come into the possession of the Templar soldiers. They are garrisoned in these and other buildings belonging to them. And with stores of arms, clothing and food they are always ready to guard the province and defend it. Below them they have stables once erected by King Solomon. They are next to the Palace, and their structure is remarkably complex. They are erected with vaults, arches and roofs of many varieties, and according to our estimation we should bear witness that they will hold ten thousand horses with their grooms. A single shot from a crossbow would hardly reach from one end of this building to the other, either in length or breadth.

'Above them the area is full of houses, dwellings and outbuildings for every kind of purpose, and it is full of walking-places, lawns, council-chambers, porches, consistories and supplies of water in splendid cisterns. Below it is equally full of wash-rooms, stores, grain rooms, stores for wood and other kinds of domestic stores.

'On the other side of the Palace, that is on the West, the Templars have built a new house, whose height, length and breadth, and all its cellars and refectories, staircase and roof, are far beyond the custom of this land. Indeed its roof is so high that, if I were to mention how high it is, those who listen would hardly believe me. There indeed they have constructed a new Palace, just as on the other side they have the old one. There too they have founded on the edge of the outer court a new church of magnificent size and workmanship.'[12]

Given that the area around the southern end of the Temple platform was in need of some repair when Baldwin vacated it, and given the extent of the Templar work carried out there, the Order would seem to have been busy, probably from almost the time they moved in. When Theoderich saw it, the Temple area was at its most developed. But, unbeknown to him, the Order's time there was limited and the new church he saw being built would never be completed.

The Loss of Jerusalem

Coming after the disaster of the Second Crusade, the fall of Ascalon can be seen as one of the high points of twelfth-century crusader campaigning. For the remainder of the 1150s and into the 1160s, the situation between Franks and Muslims would remain in something of a stalemate, seeing tit-for-tat raiding on both sides, with the Templars playing a crucial part in Christian campaigns. However, a series of events transpired in the 1160s that led the Templars to favour ploughing their own furrow when it came to matters of military tactics.

King Baldwin III died at the age of 33 in 1162 and was succeeded by his brother, the 25-year-old Amalric. Amalric's gaze was firmly fixed on Egypt and, in the autumn of 1163, he launched a campaign against Cairo.

Egypt, at the time weakened by political chaos, was seen as a fabulous prize by both Amalric and Nur ed-Din, and each was keen that it should not fall into the hands of the other. The Templars, as usual, participated in the campaign under their Grand Master, Bertrand de Blancfort, but the Egyptians forced the Franks back by breaching the dykes in the Nile Delta. Amalric was not to be kept out of Egypt for long, and he returned the following year. Whilst Amalric was negotiating with Shawar, the Egyptian vizier, Nur ed-Din attacked Antioch. With Amalric unable to return, a force led by Prince Bohemond III, which included a Templar contingent, confronted Nur ed-Din's much larger forces on 10 August 1164. Against the advice of nearly everyone – including the Templars – Bohemond ordered an attack. The Franks were routed, with 60 Templar knights perishing; only seven escaped.

Relations between the Temple and the King of Jerusalem soured even further two years later when a Templar cave-fortress in Transjordan was besieged by Nur ed-Din's troops. Amalric and his forces rushed to relieve the Templars only to meet 12 Templar knights as they were coming back across the River Jordan. The Templars explained that they had been involved in the siege and had surrendered the fortress to the Muslims. Amalric was so incensed that he ordered the Templars to be hanged. When Amalric mounted a full-scale invasion of Egypt in the autumn of 1168, the Templars refused to take part.

As has been noted earlier, the Affair of the Assassin Envoy, coming five years after the Templars' absence from the Egyptian campaign, further strained relations between the Order and the King. The following year, Amalric died. So too did Nur ed-Din. Both rulers' heirs were minors, with Amalric's son being the 13-year-old leper, Baldwin IV, while Nur ed-Din's son Malik was only 11. This led to rival claims from the *atabegs* of Damascus, Aleppo, Mosul and Cairo, and it was from Cairo that Outremer's greatest adversary emerged.

Salad ed-Din Yusuf, more commonly known as Saladin, had been one of the Muslim generals who had played a prominent part in keeping Amalric's forces at bay during the Egyptian campaigns of the 1160s, and he was to come into his own after Nur ed-Din's death by forging alliances and creating unity between the various Muslim kingdoms with the intention of continuing the *jihad* (holy war) against the Franks. As a young man, he had been more drawn towards religion, but came to feel that only a holy war would drive out the Franks, and so he became a master swordsman. Like most Muslim rulers of the time, he was also highly cultured and developed a reputation for both piety and mercy towards his enemies. Although he had his opponents within the Islamic world, he was respected by both Muslim and Christian alike, and he admired the fighting prowess of the Frankish knights. However, there was one segment of the Frankish population that he felt outright hatred for, perhaps because he understood how fanatical they were in their commitment to the Christian cause – he detested, possibly even feared, the military orders.

It was not long before the Templars engaged with forces under Saladin's control. In 1177, Saladin launched an attack against Gaza. The Templars were waiting for him. However, at the last minute, Saladin changed tack and laid siege to Ascalon instead. Baldwin IV, who had now come of age, led a counterattack. With Frankish forces concentrated at Ascalon and Gaza, Saladin, in a move reminiscent of Nur ed-Din's attack on Antioch, now decided that the relatively undefended Jerusalem would be his best option. Baldwin realised what Saladin was doing and, together with a Templar contingent from Gaza, raced after the Muslim army. They caught up with Saladin's forces at Montgisard on 25 November 1177 and destroyed them; Saladin evaded capture and escaped back to Egypt.

If Montgisard had confirmed Saladin's fear of the military might of the Templars, then the events of the summer of 1179 would show him their fanatical side. Acquiescing to pressure from the Templars, who recognised it to be a strategically important area on the road to Damascus, Baldwin had constructed a castle at Jacob's Ford on the Jordan; it was said to be the place where, according to the book of Genesis, Jacob had wrestled the angel.[13] Saladin besieged the castle, and on 10 June Templar forces under their Grand Master, Odo de St Amand, and a Christian army under Raymond of Tripoli, engaged Saladin's men. The Franks came off worse, and a number of knights were taken captive, among them Odo de St Amand. Normally, such a high-ranking Frankish noble would have been used as a bargaining tool, as had Bertrand de Blancfort when he had been captured by Nur ed-Din soon after becoming Templar Grand Master in 1156. He had been held captive for almost two years, and was released as part of a treaty signed between Byzantine Emperor Manuel Comnenus and Nur ed-Din. Odo, however, refused outright to be exchanged for a Muslim captive held by the Franks, and died in prison in 1180.

Odo's successor, Arnold of Torroja, had been Master in Spain and Provence since 1167, and was an experienced mediator. He tried to bring together the various factions in the East, knowing full well that if the Christians were split by internal disagreement, then their military strength would be fatally sapped. Saladin, a shrewd politician as well as a great commander in the field, was equally aware of potential haemorrhages amongst the Franks, and continued to consolidate his position with strategic alliances during the early 1180s, waiting for the time when Frankish disunity would signal the moment to attack. In 1184, Arnold set off for Europe with Roger des Moulins, Grand Master of the Hospital, and Patriarch Heraclius in an attempt to impress upon Western leaders the gravity of the threat posed by Saladin. Unfortunately, Arnold died before the embassy got under way, expiring at Verona on 30 September 1184, leaving Heraclius and Roger to continue the mission alone.

The man who succeeded Arnold of Torroja as Grand Master of the Temple, Gerard de Ridefort, had a reputation for rashness that exceeded even that of Odo de St Amand. He was of Flemish or Anglo-Norman origin, and was said to have joined the Order to get over a failed relationship; by 1179 he was Marshal of Jerusalem, and by 1183 he was acting as Seneschal. He was elected as Grand Master of the Temple probably in early 1185, around the time that

Baldwin IV's leprosy finally killed him at the age of 24. Despite having had a somewhat strained relationship with the monarchy since the time of Amalric, the Temple under Gerard became closely involved with the succession issue; disastrously, as it turned out.

Baldwin was succeeded by his seven-year-old nephew, who reigned as Baldwin V, with Raymond of Tripoli acting as regent, and it was in his capacity as regent that Raymond, in an attempt to gain some stability and breathing space for Outremer, agreed a truce of four years with Saladin. The boy lasted a year before he too died. Under the conditions of the leper king's 1183 will, if his nephew were to die before he reached the age of ten, then Raymond of Tripoli would continue to act as regent while a new ruler was sought by the Pope, the Holy Roman Emperor and the kings of France and England. The will, however, did not foresee the coup of September 1186 that installed Sibyl, Baldwin IV's sister, on the throne of Jerusalem as queen to her husband Guy of Lusignan's king. Chief among the conspirators that effected Guy's accession to the throne of Jerusalem was Gerard de Rideford. The Master of the Hospital, Roger des Moulins, was less enthusiastic about this weak minor French noble assuming the mantle of King of Jerusalem. The strongbox where the crown was kept was under two locks and two keys, each key being held by the Masters of the Temple and the Hospital, and it is said that on coronation day, when it was time for the strongbox to be opened in order to crown Guy, Roger threw his key out of the window, forcing Gerard to go outside to look for it.[14]

Guy was instantly unpopular. He was a weak king, who was seen by many of Outremer's vassals as being a usurper. His acceptance of the throne seriously exacerbated the factionalism among the Franks — which had played a part in his accession in the first place — and a fatal split occurred between the king and his chief allies, Gerard de Ridefort and Reginald of Chatillon on the one side, and the former regent, Raymond of Tripoli, on the other.

Reginald was, if anything, even more unpopular than Guy, and with good reason. After committing atrocities in Cyprus, then under Byzantine control, Reginald mounted an expedition to relieve Syrian Christians of their cattle. On his way back to Antioch, he was captured by Muslim forces and ransomed. No one came forward to pay up, and Reginald remained incarcerated for the next 16 years. After being released around 1176, Reginald participated — bravely, by some accounts — in the campaigns against Saladin, but he remained the Franks' loose cannon. In 1182, he had caused the maximum possible outrage in the Arab world when he had embarked upon a series of raids into Muslim territory from the Red Sea, attacking merchant ships and pilgrims on the way to Mecca; not satisfied with this, a splinter group made for Mecca, planning to dig up the body of the Prophet. Muslim forces under Saladin's brother Malik intercepted them before they reached the Holy City and wasted no time in executing them. With Guy's accession to the throne, however, Reginald was off again. Blithely disregarding Raymond's four-year truce with Saladin, Reginald attacked a large Muslim caravan; in the battle, all the caravan's Egyptian guards were slaughtered.

During late 1186 and early 1187 – around the same time that Reginald was running amok – the Templar Grand Master, Gerard de Ridefort, tried to persuade King Guy to heal the rift between himself and Raymond of Tripoli. Raymond, like Reginald, had spent time in Muslim jails, but, unlike him, had undertaken the study of Arabic and had developed an interest in Muslim culture. It was this Muslim-friendly position – adopted by the Templars themselves at other times under less maniacal Grand Masters than Gerard – that led Raymond to approach Saladin and negotiate a truce that would leave Tripoli and Galilee free from Muslim aggression whilst Raymond dealt with the ever-worsening situation with his co-religionists to the south.

The two sides agreed to attempt to broker a deal at Tiberias, which was in Raymond's territory, on the shores of the Sea of Galilee. Whilst Gerard and a Templar contingent – together with Roger des Moulins and a force of Hospitaller knights – were staying at the Templar castle of Le Fève, en route for Tiberias, Raymond sent word that he had allowed a Muslim scouting party into the area, on condition that they kept the peace. This was the red rag to Gerard's bull, and he immediately ordered an attack on the Muslims. A day or so later, on 1 May 1187, the Frankish troops encountered Saladin's men at the Springs of Cresson, north of Nazareth. Despite the fact that the Christian forces only numbered 90 Templars, with another 50 secular knights, against a Muslim strength of 7,000, Gerard ordered an attack. The Marshal of the Temple, James of Mailly, and the Master of the Hospital, Roger des

Moulins, both urged retreat, but Gerard accused them of cowardice. James of Mailly is said to have replied, 'I shall die in battle a brave man, it is you who will flee as a traitor.'[15] The Marshal's words proved to be prophetic: in the bloodbath that followed, the Christian forces were almost completely wiped out; only Gerard and two other Templars escaped with their lives.

If precipitating one military disaster was not enough, Gerard was to reprise his role as the one military adviser to whose advice one should do the exact opposite a matter of weeks later. As Saladin moved inexorably south towards Jerusalem, he took the city of Tiberias, trapping Raymond of Tripoli's wife within its walls. The Franks held a council of war at Acre on 1 July. Raymond, whose rift with King Guy was now healed, advised staying put, despite the fact that his wife was held by the enemy, as Saladin's army was too big to engage successfully. The king seemed to be in agreement until, later that night, Gerard advised an attack, convincing the king that it would be shameful to sacrifice Tiberias. Whether Gerard's advice was due to a near-suicidal streak in the Grand Master, or whether it was because he hated Raymond and couldn't bear the thought of agreeing to anything the Count of Tripoli suggested, he managed to change the king's mind.

The crusader army marched north at dawn, until it reached the village of Lubiya. They were constantly harried by Muslim archers, and were suffering greatly from thirst. The Templars, who formed the rearguard, asked if they could stop for the night. Whether the request came directly from Gerard it is not known, but King Guy agreed.

TEMPLAR CASTLES
in Syria and Palestine

La Roche de Roussel, *perhaps late 1130s*
La Roche Guillaume, *perhaps late 1130s*
Darbsak, *perhaps late 1130s*
Baghras, *perhaps late 1130s*
Port Bonnel, *perhaps late 1130s*
Antioch

La Colée, *before 1243*
Tortosa, *1152*
Chastel-Blanc, *before 1152*
al-'Arimah, *before 1152*
Tripoli

Mediterranean

Beirut
Sidon
Tyre
Beaufort, *1260*
Safad *before 1168*
Chastellet, *1178*
Acre
Haifa
Destroit, *before 1137*
Saffran *before 1172*
'Atlit, *1218*
La Fève *before 1172*
Caco, *before 1187*
Merle (Dor), *before 1187*
La Petit Gerin, *before 1187*
Caesarea

Nablus

R. Jordan

Jaffa
Castel Arnald, *1150s*
Quarantene, *before 1172*
Casal des Plains *before 1187*
Ahamant (Amman), *1166*
Toron of the Knights *before 1172*
Maldoim (Red Cistern) *before 1172*
Ascalon
Jerusalem
Gaza *1149-50*

Dead Sea

0   100 km
0   50 miles

Raymond, who was leading the vanguard, is alleged to have said when he heard this, 'Lord God, the war is over. We are dead men. The kingdom is finished.' The army was camped on an arid hill known as the Horns of Hattin and they had no water; the well was dry. During the night, Saladin's men set fire to the scrub at the foot of the hill, and the breeze carried it upwards, choking the Franks. At dawn on 4 July, Saladin's forces attacked. Crippled by the summer heat, thirst and smoke, the crusader army stood no chance. It was a disaster greater even than Cresson.

Muslim custom decrees that a man who is offered food or water shall be spared. After his capture, Saladin offered a glass of water to King Guy, who gratefully accepted it. The glass was not offered to Reginald of Chatillon, the most hated man in the whole of the East; instead, Reginald was offered the choice of conversion or death, and he re-fused to convert. Saladin wasted no more time and per-sonally decapitated him. The Templar and Hospitaller captives were given the same ultimatum – apostasy or death. Saladin's hatred of the military orders was founded upon his belief that they were the most fanatical of the Frankish warriors, and the aftermath of Hattin proved him right. The Templars were so eager for martyrdom that there was almost a stampede to be the first to be beheaded. All 230 Templar prisoners – and those of the Hospital – were executed. Only Gerard de Ridefort was spared.

After Hattin, it was only a matter of time before Jerusalem itself was in Saladin's hands. The week after Hattin, Acre fell, followed in September by Ascalon and Gaza. Finally, on 2 October 1187, Saladin entered

Jerusalem. He allowed the Church of the Holy Sepulchre to remain in Christian hands, but the cross from the Dome of the Rock was taken down and dragged through the streets where it was trampled upon and beaten with sticks. Although a small contingent of non-military Hospitallers were allowed to remain for a limited time in the Hospital to continue the work they had originally been founded for – the care of sick pilgrims – the Templars were forced to surrender their headquarters at the al-Aqsa mosque. They would never set foot there again.

The Third Crusade

Europe reacted with horror to the news that Jerusalem was lost. With Gerard de Rideford in captivity, the Templar Grand Commander Brother Terence assumed leadership of the Order, and his two letters – the first written a matter of weeks after Hattin, the second in January 1188 – described the disasters that had befallen Outremer:

> 'How many and how great the calamities with which the anger of God has permitted us to be scourged at this present time, as a consequence of our sins, we can explain neither by letters nor by tearful voice.'[16]

He goes on to write about Hattin and the loss of Acre, saying that Christian forces cannot hold out much longer 'unless we immediately receive divine aid and your [i.e. Western] help' as the infidel are 'cover[ing] the entire face of the land … like ants'.[17]

The letter was nominally addressed to Pope Urban III and to Philip of Alsace, Count of Flanders, the only major European leader who had visited the East that decade, but was also intended to be circulated as widely as possible. It reached Urban at Verona, delivered by Templar couriers, and it had a devastating effect; so much so that it probably hastened Urban's end. His successor, Gregory VIII, was already ancient and only reigned for two months, yet in that time, he called for the kings of Europe to cease fighting one another for seven years and devote themselves instead to freeing the East from the oppression of the infidel. King William II of Sicily, who, when he first heard the news, replaced his regal attire with sackcloth and went into retreat, at once sent a fleet of galleys to relieve Antioch. Something akin to the righteous furore surrounding the First Crusade began to sweep through Europe, with the Crusade being seen as a rite of passage, where one was not so much participating in order to gain absolution – as had been the case with the First Crusade – but in order to vanquish evil and prove one's courage in the field. This romanticisation reached its apogee in the monk Peter of Blois' *Passio Reginaldi*, in which the recently deceased Reginald of Chatillon is portrayed not as the murdering maniac that he was, but as a saint and martyr.

As preparations got under way in Europe for a new crusade, the Templars were at the forefront of the campaign to keep the remaining Christian possessions in the East out of Saladin's control. After the loss of Jerusalem, a fierce Christian counterattack kept Tyre in crusader hands. Several Templar castles fell, principally Safad north-west of the Sea of Galilee and Gaston, which may have been the first castle the Order took over in the Amanus March in the 1130s. The other main military order, the Hospitallers, lost Belvoir, Kerak and Montréal. But significant possessions remained – Antioch, Tyre and Tripoli all held out against Muslim forces. Both King Guy and Gerard de Ridefort were released by Saladin, and re-entered the fray.

Despite the gravity of the situation facing the Franks, the old factional disputes were still alive, as Guy found out when he attempted to re-enter Tyre. That the city held out against Saladin was largely due to the unexpected arrival of a fleet under the German prince, Conrad of Montferrat, who duly put himself in charge of the city after Saladin gave up attempting to take it in early 1188. In Conrad's eyes, the disasters of the previous year meant that Guy was no longer king. Guy's next move was against Acre, where he attempted to besiege the city in the autumn of 1189. That he was attempting to take a city at all suggests that Gerard de Ridefort had been advising him, and a contingent of Templars were among the forces that assembled around Acre. This time, Gerard's luck ran out, and he died fighting outside the walls of Acre on 4 October. When Acre was finally retaken, on 12 July 1191, the Templars had a new Grand Master and the *Reconquista* against Saladin, under the King of England, Richard the Lionheart, was finally under way.

The Third Crusade marks perhaps the highpoint between the Templars and a crusade leader. Although during the Second Crusade, the Templars had proved themselves indispensable, this was at least due in part to their financial commitment to it, and it was only with the Third Crusade that they really came into their own as a fighting force. This was in large part due to the new Grand Master, Robert de Sablé, who was a vassal and trusted friend of Richard the Lionheart. Richard, although notorious as England's absent king – he was only in the country for six months of his ten-year reign – was a brilliant military commander, ably supported by the cautious Robert. Within two months of Acre, Richard's tactical skill would show its hand.

On 7 September 1191 Saladin attacked the crusader army as it marched south from Caesarea, just outside the forest of Arsuf. During the march, the Templars had formed the rearguard, while the Hospitallers complemented them at the front of the column. During the battle itself, Richard reversed the roles of the orders to great effect, knowing that he could rely on their discipline in the field. Although Muslim losses were light, it was Saladin's first defeat since the victory at Hattin, and it marked a turning point for the Crusade. It brought renewed hope to the coastal cities still under Christian control that Jerusalem itself could be retaken.

The Third Crusade, however, was not to retake the Holy City. Although Richard came within sight of its walls, both Robert de Sablé and the Hospitaller Grand Master Geoffroi de Donjon urged caution, pointing out that even if Jerusalem could be taken, retaining it after the departure of the crusaders would be difficult, if not impossible. Richard agreed with the Grand Masters, and decided his next course of action would be to refortify Ascalon.

Richard was keen to return to England, to deal with his

increasingly troublesome brother John. His main priority before he left, therefore, was to ensure that the succession issue was decided. His own favoured candidate was Guy of Lusignan, but he was outvoted by the kingdom's barons, who wanted Conrad of Montferrat to be the next King of Jerusalem instead. Conrad, however, was murdered by the Assassins in the streets of Acre, leaving the way open for Richard's nephew, Henry of Champagne, to succeed. (Some have suspected Richard of ordering Conrad's death, but this is disputed.) This left the former king, Guy of Lusignan, to be dealt with, and it was decided that he should be given Cyprus, an island that had been a thorn in the sides of both Richard and the Templars.

When Richard was en route to Outremer in early 1191, two of his ships had ended up on Cyprus. The island was then under the control of Isaac Ducas Comnenus, a particularly slippery Byzantine prince who had just made a pact with Saladin. The first of Richard's ships had contained crusaders, while the second carried Richard's betrothed, Berengaria of Navarre, and her chaperone, his sister Joan, the Dowager Queen of Sicily. Richard arrived a week later and demanded the release of the prisoners. Isaac refused, and Richard, perhaps seeing Cyprus as a source of useful booty for the Third Crusade, launched an attack against Isaac's forces. The Byzantine, hated by the islanders, was quickly overpowered and a Western garrison was installed on the island. After Richard had left for the Holy Land, word reached him that the local population was proving difficult to control, and the new Templar Grand Master, Robert de Sablé – who was almost certainly elected to the position at Richard's behest – offered to buy the island from Richard for 100,000 *besants*. Richard agreed, and a Templar garrison left for the island. However, they too had trouble with the locals, culminating in their fort at Nicosia being besieged on 4 April 1192, and realised that, without a larger garrison, holding the island would be a thankless task. They therefore sold it back to Richard. Richard felt that this would be the ideal place to put the habitually in-effectual Guy, and sold the island to him for 60,000 *besants*, making the former king now Guy of Cyprus in the process.

Saladin proved to be less easy to dispose of, and negoti-ations dragged on. In an attempt to force him to come to terms, the Franks successfully attacked the castle of Daron, which lay to the south of Ascalon. Richard returned to Acre just as Saladin made a surprise move against Jaffa, tak-ing the town after three days. Richard, accompanied by only 80 knights – Templars amongst them – 400 archers and 2,000 Italian mercenaries, improvised a counterattack and beat off the much larger Muslim force. Negotiations were concluded not long after. Richard agreed to demolish Ascalon, while Saladin agreed to recognise Christian pos-sessions along the coast. Furthermore, Christians and Muslims were to be allowed to cross each other's territory, and Christian pilgrims were free to visit Jerusalem and the Holy Places.

On 9 October 1192, Richard left the Holy Land with a Templar escort. He never returned. Saladin died the fol-lowing year. A tenuous peace descended on the Lands Beyond the Sea.

The Templars at the turn of the Thirteenth Century

The Templars, like much of the Latin East after the Third Crusade, found themselves trying to rebuild the hold they had had before the disasters of the late 1180s. Despite the fact that Christian pilgrims were allowed into Jerusalem, they themselves were not, and so they established new headquarters at Acre, which now became the most important city in the Latin East, and the Templars' base for the next 100 years. The Order had had a presence in the city for decades, and the German monk Theoderich saw it in the 1170s. The chronicler known as the Templar of Tyre, writing in the mid-thirteenth century, described it as:

> 'The strongest place of the city, largely situated along the seashore, like a castle. At its entrance it had a high and strong tower, the wall of which was 28 feet thick. On each side of the tower was a smaller tower, and on each of these was a gilded lion passant, as large as an ox. These four lions [together with] the gold and the labour, cost 1,500 Saracen *besants*, and were noble to look upon. On the other side, near the Street of the Pisans, there was another tower, and near this tower on the Street of St Anne, was a large and noble palace, which was the Master's. In front of the house of the nuns of St Anne was another high tower, which had bells, and a very noble and high church. There was another ancient tower on the seashore, which Saladin had built 100 years before, in which the Temple kept its treasure, and it was so close to the sea that the waves

washed against it. Within the Temple area there were other beautiful and noble houses, which I will not describe here.'[18]

Although Acre, long familiar to the Order, proved to be a sound choice of location for their new base of operations, it was the Templars' attempts to re-establish themselves in the Amanus March, which had been amongst their very first fortified possessions in the East, that illustrate how much damage had been done by Saladin's campaigns.

The Templar castles Gaston (Baghras) and Darbsaq had both fallen to Saladin's forces during September 1188, severely weakening the Order's powerbase in the region. Gaston proved to be a drain on resources, however, and, in 1191, the Muslims abandoned it. Prince Leo of Cilician Armenia then occupied and refortified it. When the Templars attempted to gain access to the fortress, they were refused, and so began a long campaign to wrest control of it from Leo. The situation was made infinitely more complicated by Leo's war with Antioch, the precarious position of the Armenian Church and the rival claims made by Leo's descendants and those of his Antiochene rival, Bohemond III. An intermittent campaign was conducted between the Templars and Leo's forces until 1211, when, in a series of attacks on the Templars and their holdings, the recently elected Grand Master, Guillame de Chartres, was wounded and Pope Innocent III subsequently excommunicated Leo. The Armenian Church had only been reconciled with Rome since 1197, and Leo evidently felt that his excommunication put him politically beyond the pale, so he restored Gaston and other Templar holdings to the Order between 1213 and 1216.

The sense of the Order – and Christendom – re-establishing itself after the end of the Third Crusade is also evident in the actions of Pope Innocent III (1198–1216). In 1199, he wrote to the leaders of Outremer complaining that no one seemed to have the heart for a new crusade (which he himself was very keen to promote). He also published a series of bulls that reiterated the Templars' special status, and demanded that the clergy respect the Order's rights and privileges. He reminded the clergy in no uncertain terms that the Templars had a right to their own burial grounds and had the freedom to erect churches on their own land and warned them against doing violence to any serving brother or to Templar property. Furthermore, the clergy were asked not to forget that the Templars were exempt from paying tithes, that they should be left in peace to collect those tithes due to them from their own lands, and that the clergy were expressly forbidden to divert any of these funds their way; the clergy were also not to excommunicate Templar churches and those who broke into Templar houses were to be punished; the clergy were to prevent brothers who were serving in the Order for a set period of time from leaving early; bishops who forced Templars to fight other Christians (as happened in parts of the Iberian peninsula and eastern Europe) were condemned; and the clergy were instructed to protect the property and privileges of the Templars against usurpers, and were to excommunicate those who disobeyed. Just in case the clergy did not get the point, Innocent also reissued the bull that had given the Templars their privileges in the first place, *Omne datum optimum*.

Innocent also directly addressed the Order, warning its members not to abuse any of their privileges, knowing full well that they were often accused of the sin of pride. He complained that they gave full Christian burial to anybody, as long as they had some money to pay for it, not bothering to find out whether they had been excommunicated or had some other reason for not being allowed to be laid to rest in consecrated ground. In prophetic words, Innocent warned the Order that if they did not change their ways, they would become agents of the Devil.

The Other Military Orders

One unexpected development in the Latin East after the end of the Third Crusade was the establishment of a new military order. In 1197, German crusaders had arrived in the East; they were largely unsuccessful, their sole military contribution being their participation in the capture of Beirut that year. Most of the German crusaders returned home, but a number of knights remained in the East, and joined a field hospital that had been set up in 1190 by merchants from Bremen and Lübeck. During the siege of Acre in 1191 they were said to have welcomed brothers from the Hospital of St Mary of the Germans, which, tradition holds, was founded in Jerusalem in 1127. The new hospital's first base in Acre was a tent on the shore made from a ship's mainsail. When the knights joined, they became the Teutonic Knights of St Mary's

Hospital of Jerusalem, and on 5 March 1198, the Teutonic Knights were accepted as an order of the church at the Temple compound in Acre.

The Teutonic Knights were the last of the three great military orders to be founded. The first of them, the Hospitallers, had been founded before the formation of the Templars, sometime around 1070. The Hospital – founded by a group of merchants from Amalfi – was originally that of St John the Almoner, and it operated an infirmary and guest house for pilgrims near the Church of Holy Sepulchre. The first Grand Master was Peter Gerard, who was elected in about 1100. As soon as the Kingdom of Jerusalem was established, Godfroi de Bouillon donated lands to the Order, and many others followed suit, with the result that the Hospitallers had extensive holdings in Europe as well as the East. The capture of Jerusalem in 1099 led naturally to the influx of a greater number of pilgrims than ever, and it was decided that a more prominent patron saint should be adopted for the Order: John the Almoner was replaced by John the Baptist. The Hospital was recognised as an order by Pope Paschal II (1099–1118) in 1113.

The Order's second Grand Master, Raymond de Puy, oversaw the Hospital's adoption of an increasingly military role. In the early years, it is possible that Templars were used to guard the Hospital's establishments, but during the 1120s it seems that the Hospitallers themselves started to militarise. A Hospitaller constable is mentioned in documents dating from 1126,[19] but the first firm date for military activity is 1136, when King Fulk gave the Order the castle of Gibelin, on the Gaza–Hebron road. Like the Templars, the Hospitallers received papal privileges: Innocent II (1130–43) forbade bishops to interdict Hospitaller chapels; Anastasius IV (1153–54) gave them their own priests; while Adrian IV (1154–59) gave them their own churches. Their rule evolved slowly, with Raymond being guided by pragmatic concerns. Like the Teutonic Knights after them, some of the Hospital's statutes were modelled on those of the Templars.

In addition to the Hospital and the Teutonic Knights, there were several smaller orders active in the East. The Hospital of St Lazarus was the third military order to be founded after the Temple and the Hospital of St John. Originating probably from a Greek or Armenian leper house in Jerusalem, the Order was set up solely for knights who had contracted leprosy. It was taken over by the Hospital of St John during the early 1100s, and it is said that the first Hospitaller Grand Master, Peter Gerard, also acted as the Grand Master of St Lazarus. According to legend, all their subsequent Grand Masters were lepers. They established a chain of houses for lepers across the East and Europe, which became known as 'Lazar Houses', and were chiefly known for their hospitaller work, although they participated in a number of engagements in the East alongside the Templars and Hospitallers. The Templar Rule demanded that a brother who caught leprosy must transfer to the Order of St Lazarus.[20]

The Knights of Our Lady of Montjoie were recognised as an order by a bull issued by Pope Alexander III (1159–81) in 1180. The Order was founded by a Spanish knight, Count Rodrigo, taking its name from the castle of Montjoie just outside of Jerusalem (the name itself deriving from the cries of joy that pilgrims were said to have uttered upon first seeing the Holy City). The Order – never numerous at the best of times – seemed to have had trouble gaining recruits, and, after the disasters of 1187, the surviving brothers retired to Aragon, where they changed their name to the Order of Trufac.

The Hospitallers of St Thomas of Canterbury, also known as the Knights of St Thomas Acon, were founded around the same time as the Teutonic Knights. Their origins were also from the time of the Third Crusade: William, the Dean of St Paul's, was so moved by the plight of the English crusaders that, after the capture of Acre in 1191, he bought a small chapel and cemetery. The hospital that he founded was restricted to Englishmen, although many preferred to join the Templars and the Hospitallers instead. Like their better-known contemporaries, they received donations of land in the East and in Europe. They are thought to have militarised around the time of the Fifth Crusade.

Military Tactics

The Templars' reputation in the field was unsurpassed. When the Franks were crushed at Hattin, Saladin ordered that all the captive Templars and Hospitallers be executed, such was his conviction that the military orders were the Franks' main weapon against Islam. (Indeed, Saladin viewed the two orders as 'impure races'.[21])

The Templars – as did the secular Franks – employed

cavalry and infantry. The former comprised mounted knights and sergeants, the latter archers and troops armed with axes and spears. The knights were the mediaeval equivalent of a tank, with their great war horses often standing up to 17 hands high. The horses – known as destriers – were taught to kick, butt and bite. The sergeants were also mounted, but wore lighter armour and rode in the rear.

Tactics were simple, but, when timed properly, were devastatingly effective. Initially, the infantry would provide cover, before the cavalry charge, which would form the main attack. A properly timed charge would wipe out everything in its path; misjudged charges led to disasters such as the Springs of Cresson. During the melée, the Templars were sworn to stay in the field as long as the Order's distinctive black and white banner, known as the *beauseant*, remained aloft. As soon as the *beauseant* was lost to sight, the Templars would rally to the Hospitaller banner or, if that too was down, then any remaining Christian banner. Their vows meant that they were usually the first into the field, and the last to leave.

In the early years of the Latin East, the Templars quickly developed a fearsome reputation as the best-trained soldiers the Franks had, showing almost suicidal bravery at times. This reached an apogee during the Mastership of Gerard de Ridefort, who died during a reckless attack at Acre. However, as the twelfth century gave way to the thirteenth, the Templars began to retreat from their earlier zeal and grew ever more cautious in battle.

The Temple and the Empire

Innocent's plans for a new crusade in the East finally materialised in 1218, although he himself did not live to see it. After Innocent's death in July 1216, he was succeeded by Honorius III (1216–27), who was determined to get the crusading machinery in motion. Although the Templars had played little or no role in the Fourth Crusade (1202–04) – mainly due to the crusade's failure to actually make it to Palestine after sacking Constantinople – they were heavily involved in the Fifth from the outset.

A crusade fund was established at the Paris Temple, where the Templar treasurer, Brother Haimard, oversaw donations. Honorius wrote to the Templar Grand Master, Guillaume de Chartres, and also to his opposite number in the Hospital, Garin de Montaigu, ordering them to meet the crusade's leaders, King Andrew of Hungary and Leopold, Duke of Austria, on Cyprus. As things turned out, the two men and their respective armies arrived separately in the East in the autumn of 1217. Initial plans to attack Damascus were shelved after the somewhat lacklustre campaign of November 1217 in favour of mounting a campaign in Egypt, with the intention of capturing the key city of Damietta. With reinforcements under the King of Jerusalem, John of Brienne (1210–25), the crusaders – including contingents of Templars, Hospitallers and Teutonic Knights – landed at Damietta in June 1218. It was here that the Templar Grand Master, who had been unwell since the previous autumn, died, and was succeeded by Garin de Montaigu's brother, Peter. For the first and only time, the

Orders of the Temple and the Hospital were under the control of the same family. (A third brother, Eustorge, was Archbishop of Nicosia.)

Damietta was swiftly captured. Oliver of Paderborn, the master of Cologne's cathedral school, who went on the Fifth Crusade, wrote in admiration of the Templars' ability to fight in the waterlogged terrain of the Nile Delta, using both a fleet of ships and pontoons, and being able to negotiate the swamps on horseback. Warfare of this sort would not normally be waged in the sun-baked hills and valleys of Palestine, and that the Templars were so effective in the capture of Damietta proved that they were military strategists and engineers of genius.

The crusaders' initial success moved the Egyptian Sultan, al-Kamil, Saladin's brother, to offer them Jerusalem in return for Damietta. Pelagius, the Papal legate and self-appointed leader of the Crusade, rejected the offer. As with Richard and the question of Jerusalem on the Third Crusade, the Montaigu brothers had argued that Jerusalem could not be held unless the lands beyond the Jordan were also ceded to the crusaders, and this was something that was not part of al-Kamil's offer. They decided to wait for further reinforcements before continuing with the Crusade, believing that the cause would be greatly aided by the arrival of the Holy Roman Emperor, Frederick II. When it became apparent that an Imperial army was not going to materialise, Pelagius ordered an advance up the Nile. The Templars were reluctant, believing that the Crusade's resources were overstretched. Their misgivings proved to be correct. When the Frankish army reached the town of

Mansurah, al-Kamil's forces cut off the crusaders' rear and blocked their path ahead by opening the sluice gates; the Crusade was literally flooded into submission. Pelagius had no choice but to accept al-Kamil's terms and surrender Damietta. A truce of eight years was also agreed.

Despite Frederick's failure to appear, the general feeling remained that he would fulfil his vow to go on crusade, a vow he had taken at his coronation in Frankfurt in 1212. The grandson of Frederick Barbarossa, who had died while on the Third Crusade in 1190, Frederick II was one of the most extraordinary characters of his age. He was raised in Sicily and was elected king at the age of three. He had a naturally enquiring mind, and became fluent in not just Italian, French and German, but also Greek, Latin and Arabic. In choosing to rule from Sicily, Frederick created a political and cultural gap that was far wider than the straits of Messina, which separated the island from the Italian mainland, might suggest: he had a pronounced interest in Arabic culture, and his bodyguard was made up entirely of Saracens. He was rumoured to be an atheist, and certainly had what might be termed a scientific outlook on nature, which led to a number of bizarre and sometimes cruel experiments: children were raised in complete silence in order to observe what language they would utter when they were old enough to talk (this would therefore prove what language Adam and Eve had spoken in the Garden of Eden[22]); a man was imprisoned in a wine barrel to see if his soul could be seen departing from his body at the moment of death; two men – one indolent, the other active – were killed and then dissected in order to find out how their lifestyles had affected their internal organs. Rumours abounded about Frederick's private life, and he certainly seems to have had somewhat liberal attitudes to sex. He defended the Jews of Germany against charges of the ritual murder of Christian children, and, at one point, is said to have seriously considered converting to Islam, which would have made him, as Holy Roman Emperor, neither holy, Roman nor emperor.

Frederick and his army finally landed at Acre on 7 September 1228. It had been a difficult passage: Frederick's forces had to put in at Otranto because of illness; and this delay had enraged the new pope, Gregory IX, so much that he excommunicated the Emperor. When he finally set sail again the following spring, Frederick was excommunicated again for attempting to go on crusade while excommunicated. Frederick was not unduly bothered by this, but, by the time he reached Acre that autumn, word of his excommunications had spread among the clergy and baronage of Outremer. This officially meant that Frederick could no longer command the Crusade, and the Latins were split along Papal–Imperial lines. Most of the Frankish barons, the Templars and the Hospitallers sided with the Pope – the Templars, after all, were answerable to none save the pontiff himself – while the Teutonic Knights sided with Frederick. Furthermore, Frederick's wife, Isabel, had died giving birth to their son Conrad that May, and, as his claim to the crown of Jerusalem was through his marriage to her, he was technically no longer king either, merely the regent for the infant Conrad.

Perhaps because of his dubious status as both leader of

the Sixth Crusade and as King of Jerusalem, Frederick began to assert his authority by marching to 'Atlīt and demanding that the Templars hand the castle over to a German garrison (presumably to be placed under the control of the Teutonic Knights). The Templars refused to let Frederick in and he returned to Acre. His next move was to march on Jaffa. The Templars and the Hospitallers would not accept Frederick's command, and followed the Imperial forces a day's journey behind. By the time they had reached Arsuf, Frederick delegated his command to his generals, therefore making it possible for the two main military orders to rejoin the Crusade. Now expecting to engage the enemy, the Templars were to be frustrated by a coup of staggering proportions – Frederick regained Jerusalem through diplomacy.

The recovery of the Holy City came as a complete surprise to the military orders and to the barons of Outremer; to Frederick, however, it was something he had possibly been expecting. Even before he left Sicily, Frederick had received the Emir Fakhr ad-Din ibn as-Shaikh, al-Kamil's ambassador, at court in Palermo; the Emir brought the Emperor news that al-Kamil would return Jerusalem to Christian control if Frederick promised to help the Sultan in his campaign to recapture Damascus. Frederick had not given al-Kamil a definite answer, and, during the negotiations conducted while on crusade, the subject had naturally come up again. By this time, however, Frederick had received news that the situation back home had taken a severe turn for the worse, with war breaking out between an Imperial army under Reginald of Spoleto, and a papal army under the former King of Jerusalem, John of Brienne, and he was anxious to return to Palermo. Although the thought of a successful Christian–Muslim alliance against al-Kamil's enemies in Damascus might have appealed to Frederick's ego, it would have been the greatest outrage of all time in the eyes of the Pope and Western leaders; quite what would have happened is difficult to imagine. A compromise was therefore reached in which Frederick and al-Kamil saved face – Jerusalem was returned to the Franks, but the Temple Mount was to remain in Muslim control. The city itself was to remain undefended, being connected to the coastal cities by a thin corridor of land. The military orders were forbidden from carrying out reinforcements on their castles, and a ten-year truce between the two leaders was agreed.

Despite this historic achievement, the recovery of Jerusalem led to the pious on both sides of accusing their respective leaders of treachery, and it very nearly led to a civil war among the Franks. Frederick was crowned King of Jerusalem in the Church of the Holy Sepulchre on 17 March 1229, despite the fact that the city had been placed under interdict by the Patriarch of Jerusalem, Gerold of Lausanne, should the Emperor arrive. The interdict forbade any church ceremonies from taking place whilst Frederick was within the walls of the city, but it made no difference – with no priests to crown him, Frederick simply crowned himself. The Templars and the Hospitallers stayed away, leaving only the loyal Teutonic Knights to guard the Emperor and King. Their great Grand Master, Herman von Salza, delivered an oration in which Frederick forgave the Pope for opposing him (a none too subtle reference to Frederick's double excommunication), and promised to do everything he could to defend the Church and the Empire. Frederick signed himself God's 'Vicar on Earth', a title which was normally reserved for the pontiff, thus throwing down the gauntlet. For Frederick, the enemy was not al-Kamil, but the Papacy.

After the ceremony, Frederick made a tour of Jerusalem. With typical Muslim diplomacy, al-Kamil had ordered the *muezzins* not to call the faithful to prayer while Frederick was in the city. Frederick, however, apparently wanted to hear the prayer-call – citing it as his reason for coming to Jerusalem – and when he entered the Dome of the Rock, he threw out a priest who had attempted to enter with the Imperial entourage, threatening to pluck out the man's eyes if he attempted it again. Frederick then noticed a wooden lattice that had been placed over a window inside the Dome. It was explained to him that it had been placed there to keep the sparrows out, and Frederick, using the disparaging Muslim term for the Franks, replied, 'God has now sent you pigs.'

It was when Frederick returned to Acre that the 'pigs' nearly rose against him. He found Gerold and the Templars assembling forces to wrest Jerusalem from his control and attack Damascus. A tense stand-off ensued outside the city walls. It descended into a slanging match, with Frederick hurling insults at both the Patriarch and the Templars, in particular the Grand Master, Peter de Montaigu. Things had reached a spectacular all-time low in Templar–Imperial relations, so much so that both the Grand Master and the

Emperor were each concerned for their physical safety. According to the chronicler Philip of Novara, Frederick was planning to kidnap a number of Frankish barons – and Peter de Montaigu – and have them tried at a kangaroo court before having them executed. Counter-propaganda circulated that the Templars were planning to assassinate Frederick whilst he was in Jerusalem, and the Emperor, possibly aware of the plot, only spent two nights in the city. Before Frederick left the Holy Land, he attempted to storm the Temple compound in Acre without success. When he finally did leave, at dawn on 1 May 1229, the jeering crowds pelted him with dung.

Frederick's return to the West did not mark the end of his involvement in the affairs of Outremer. In 1231, his *bailli*, or representative, Richard Filangieri, arrived with an Imperial force and tried to seize Acre. Although unsuccessful, he did manage to establish a base at Tyre, where he remained a thorn in the side of the Templars and the anti-Frederick camp. In 1232, the new Templar Grand Master, Armand de Périgord, was one of those who attempted to mediate between Filangieri and aggrieved Frankish barons, but the attempt at reconciliation failed.

For the remainder of the 1230s, the Templars found themselves mainly concerned with local disputes, such as mounting campaigns against local warlords like the Sultan of Hamah when he failed to pay his annual tribute (protection money, in modern parlance), or Muslim foragers who came too close to the Templar stronghold of 'Atlīt. It was only the imminent ending of the ten-year truce between Frederick and al-Kamil that brought the Templars back into the wider sphere, and saw them once again adopt an anti-Imperial stance.

As 1239 approached, Pope Gregory preached a new crusade, knowing how vulnerable Jerusalem was and fearful that Latin possessions could be wiped off the map altogether. Only one minor French noble, Theobald, Count of Champagne, took the Cross. He arrived in the East on 1 September 1239 and, like the participants of the Second Crusade before him, immediately failed to grasp the complexities of the political situation in Outremer. He found that the Franks, encouraged by the Templars, had made an alliance with the ruler of Damascus – in return for helping the Damascene forces against the Egyptians, various lands seized by the Muslims would be returned to Christian control. (This included the great Templar fortress of Safad, which had been lost at Hattin, and the Order immediately began restoring it to its former strength.) Theobald was evidently unaware that al-Kamil had died in March of the previous year, resulting in anarchy in the Muslim world as his heirs and claimants fought amongst themselves for al-Kamil's title. A breakaway force under Henry, Count of Bar, decided to take advantage of the situation by attacking Egypt; they were decimated at Gaza. The blame fell not on Henry for underestimating the size of the Egyptian army, but on the Templars and Hospitallers – who had correctly assessed the danger posed by the Egyptian forces – for refusing to support him.

Another crusade arrived the following year, under the leadership of Richard, Duke of Cornwall. Richard, nephew of the Lionheart, brother of Henry III of England

and brother-in-law of the Emperor, clearly hoped to make an impact, and immediately set to work trying to free Christian prisoners from both Damascus and Cairo and to get the lands recently ceded to the Franks officially recognised by all parties. Richard's success was not to last. As soon as he had sailed for England, the Templars – unimpressed by Richard's efforts and suspicious of Egyptian duplicity – attacked the city of Hebron, then under Egyptian control, followed by the recapture of Nablus.

With Richard gone, the Templars found themselves in open conflict, not just with Imperial forces under Frederick's *bailli*, Richard Filangieri, but also with the Hospitallers. Although rivalry between the two Orders had always existed, settlements were usually found before any serious damage could be mutually inflicted. This time, however, the Hospital had opposed the Templars' attack on Hebron and Nablus, favouring, like Richard of Cornwall, diplomacy with the Egyptians. With the Duke of Cornwall safely bound for home, Filangieri tried to capture Acre, using the Hospital compound there as his base. The Templars, once more adopting the militant anti-Imperialist stance they had taken under Peter de Montaigu, responded by participating in the subsequent attack on the Hospitaller headquarters, besieging it for six months. The situation came to a head with the arrival in the East of Thomas of Aquino, the Count of Acerra, to accept the crown of Jerusalem on behalf of Frederick's son Conrad, who had now come of age. The Templar Grand Master, Armand de Périgord, was one of those who strongly opposed Conrad's accession, and instead lent support to Alice, Dowager

Queen of Cyprus, on the grounds that she was the nearest heir and was therefore the only legitimate candidate for the Regency of Jerusalem. Genoese and Venetian forces arrived and, in the summer of 1243, they helped the Franks in evicting Filangieri, Count Thomas and all the rest of the Imperial party from Tyre, claiming – with dubious legality – that Conrad's claim to the throne of Jerusalem was invalid as he had not appeared in person to claim the crown.

The Franks had no time to put their house in order before a new crisis loomed, when, in early 1244, war broke out once again between Egypt and Damascus. This time, Egyptian forces were bolstered by the Khorezmian Turks, a tribe of ferocious nomads of mercenary persuasion. They flooded south from their base in Edessa and, on 11 July, attacked Jerusalem. The city finally fell a month later, on 23 August. The bones of Godfroi de Bouillon and other Kings of Jerusalem were disinterred and the Church of the Holy Sepulchre was set alight. Jerusalem would never again be under Christian control. But worse was to follow.

The Khorezmians headed south, joining forces with the Egyptian army at Gaza. On 17 October at La Forbie, the Frankish forces attacked the combined Muslim forces. It was a disaster; the Damascenes deserted and the remaining Christian forces were slaughtered, with at least 800 being taken prisoner and sold into slavery in Egypt. Among them was the Templar Grand Master, Armand de Périgord, who disappeared into the bowels of an Egyptian jail and was never seen again. The Order also lost somewhere between 260 and 300 knights; only 33 Templars, 26 Hospitallers and three Teutonic Knights returned from the field. The following year, Damascus fell to the Egyptians, and it seemed that Outremer's final hour had come.

The Fall of Acre

La Forbie was a disaster almost on par with Hattin. The West was shocked, and the possibility of a new crusade was considered. The only monarch who actually arrived in the East was Louis IX, the saintly French king, who had nearly died of fever around the same time that the Franks were being cut down on the field of La Forbie. His recovery, and the news that the East was once again in dire peril, decided the matter for him. After extensive preparations, he sailed from Aigues-Mortes in the Camargue on 25 August 1248, arriving on Cyprus on 17 September. Among the welcoming party was the new Templar Grand Master, Guillame de Sonnac, who had been elected after the Order's failure to secure the release of Armand de Périgord from captivity in Egypt.[23]

The crusaders landed in Egypt on 5 June 1249, and found to their surprise that Damietta had been evacuated. They managed to take the city the following day, with the loss of only one life. Louis decided to march south towards Cairo, using the Templars to form the vanguard. Things seemed to be going the way of the Franks, a feeling reinforced when, on 23 November, the Egyptian Sultan, al-Sālih Aiyūb, died. However, they then spent a month trying to cross a branch of the Nile, but could not find a suitable place until a local Bedouin showed them the ford. On 8 February 1250, they began to cross, with the Templars and

Richard, Count of Artois, Louis' brother, and William Longespée, the Earl of Salisbury, heading the column. It was at this point that things began to go badly wrong. On arriving on the opposite bank of the river, Richard decided to attack the Muslims rather than wait for the rest of the crusaders to finish crossing the river, and forced the Muslims to retreat to the nearby town of Mansurah. The Templars were angry at what they saw as Richard's arrogation of their role, and passed a message to the Count to that effect. However, Foucaud du Merle, the knight who was holding the bridle of Richard's horse, was deaf, and failed to pass the message on. Richard charged off in pursuit of the Muslim forces and the Templars, now concerned at saving face, chased after him, determined to regain their position in the van. The Christian forces poured into Mansurah and found themselves trapped by wooden beams and other debris that had been used to close off the narrow streets. In the ensuing chaos, 300 knights died and 280 Templars; the instigator of the ill-fated attack, Richard of Artois, drowned under the weight of his armour while trying to swim to safety, while the Templar Grand Master Guillame de Sonnac lost an eye. On 11 February, there was a second onslaught in which Guillame lost his other eye and died later the same day. Although the Muslim forces were driven back, it became clear that taking Mansurah would not be easy.

Louis decided to sit it out, and waited. While the army was entrenched outside the walls of Mansurah, the Muslims had managed to cut the crusaders' supply lines from Damietta, depriving them of fresh food. To make matters worse, disease was spreading rapidly through the Frankish army. Louis suffered from acute dysentery and was continually visiting the latrine; indeed, so frequent were the king's visits that, according to the chronicler Joinville, his servants aided matters by cutting away the lower part of his drawers. Louis realised that he would have to negotiate, but the offer was rejected. On 5 April, the Franks began to retreat. The Muslims came after them and the casualties on the Christian side ran to several thousand. Only 14 survived from the military orders, including three Templars. As a final humiliation, most of the army – including Louis himself – was captured. Damietta was to be handed over in return for the king's life; the rest of the captives were to be ransomed for half a million *livres*.

Damietta was returned to Muslim control and, on 6 May, Louis was released. Before he left Egypt, there was still the matter of paying the rest of the ransom, and counting began on 7 May. By the end of the following day, it was apparent that they were still 30,000 *livres* short. Joinville suggested to the king that the amount be borrowed from the Templars, and Louis agreed. Joinville went to the Templars to ask for the money, but the Order's commander, Stephen of Otricourt, refused to hand the sum over on the grounds that he could only release the money to the people who had deposited it in the first place. Tempers began to fray and 'there were many hard and abusive words'[24] between Joinville and the Commander until the Templar Marshal, Reginald de Vichiers, suggested that, although they had sworn vows to protect their clients' money, there was nothing stopping Joinville from taking the money by force. Therefore, with the king's permission, Joinville went on board the Templar galley where the money was kept in the hold. However, the Templar treasurer refused to open the strongbox, perhaps owing to Joinville's somewhat haggard appearance after the deprivations of the retreat from Mansurah and also to the fact that he was wielding an axe. At this point, Reginald de Vichiers, clearly concerned that Joinville was about to commit an act of violence, intervened and ordered the treasurer to open the strongbox and hand the money over.

Louis arrived back in Acre on 13 May, and, with his support, Reginald de Vichiers was elected Grand Master of the Temple. This was partially to repay Reginald for his role in the king's release, but also for his involvement with the Crusade from its inception: as early as 1246, Reginald was acting on behalf of Louis in arranging shipping to carry the crusaders to the East. Louis stayed in Outremer for another four years, and he initially remained on close terms with the Templars. Indeed, when a son was born to Louis, the baby was delivered in the castle of 'Atlīt, and Reginald acted as his godfather. Relations were soon strained, however, when Reginald attempted to form a new alliance with Damascus without consulting Louis. The king was furious, and made the Grand Master perform public penance for his insubordination.

Louis left the East in April 1254. Despite the failure in Egypt, the Crusade had achieved a number of things: fortifications were improved in key cities such as Caesarea, Jaffa, Sidon and Acre itself, and Louis pledged to assist in maintaining them by supplying a constant garrison of

French troops. The inland castles – such as Safad – were all in the hands of the military orders, as they had proved too expensive for the secular baronage to run. Additionally, Louis had shown that Outremer could still be governed well provided that it had a single, strong leader behind whom the Frankish barons could unite. And in his six years in the East, he had injected a vast amount of money into the economy – 1.3 million *livres tournois*, about 11 or 12 times the annual income of his kingdom.[25]

When Louis left, he took his leadership and financial support with him. Unfortunately for the Franks, this coincided almost exactly with the rise of two new powers that would both threaten Outremer – the Mongols and the Mamluks. Of the two, the Mongols proved the most immediate threat. Indeed, such was the Frankish fear of them that it brought all three of the main military orders together. The Templars, Hospitallers and Teutonic Knights all agreed to put their habitual squabbles to one side in the name of defending Outremer (an achievement all the more impressive when one considers that civil war had broken out in the East shortly after Louis' departure, with the Templars and Teutonic Knights on one side, and the Hospitallers on the other). Letters were written and frantically dispatched to the West. One Templar courier managed to make it to London in just 13 weeks, bearing a doom-laden account of the situation in the East, reminiscent of the letters of Brother Terence after the disasters of 1187:

'... when they had read these letters, both the king [Henry III] and the Templars ... gave way to lamentation

Templar Preceptories and
Castles in the 12th Century

North Sea

*Atlantic
Ocean*

Mediterranean Sea

Temple

Clontarf

Willoughton

Temple
Cowley
Temple Guiting
Templecombe
Shipley

Temple
Dinsley
Cressing
London

Sommereux
Laon
Beauvais
Paris
La Neuville
Orléans
Coulours
Nantes
Marmoutier
La Rochelle

Rodez
Richerenches
La Selve
Roaix
Saint-Gilles
Avignon
Albenga
Montsaunès
Pézenas
Arles
Siena
Monzón
Douzens
Chalamera
Mas-Deu
Rome
Braga
Grañera
Novillas
Palau
Soure
Ambel
Remolins
Barbara
Tomar
Corbins
Almourol
Santarém

0		250 km	500 km
0	150 miles	300 miles	

and sadness, on a scale no one had ever seen before. For the news was that the Tartars [Mongols], advancing with an innumerable force, had already occupied and devastated the Holy Land almost up to Acre ... unless help is quickly brought, a horrible annihilation will swiftly be visited upon the world.'[26]

On 3 September 1260, a horrible annihilation was indeed visited upon Outremer, but it was not the Franks who bore the brunt of it: it was the Mongols themselves. At 'Ain Jūlāt, south of Nazareth, a Mongol army was crushed by Mamluk forces under the sultan Saif-ad-Dīn Kutuz. The Mamluks, a caste of elite slave warriors who had been a permanent component of the Egyptian military for a century, had recently seized power in Egypt, bringing to an end the rule of Saladin's descendants. Kutuz himself was soon ousted, being assassinated the month following the victory at 'Ain Jūlāt. He was replaced as sultan by Baybars, who had fought in the Egyptian army at La Forbie and against Louis at Mansurah; he would do more damage to the Franks than any other Muslim leader since Saladin.

Baybars immediately set about destroying Frankish possessions in Outremer. The 1260s are a litany of Christian defeats, with even such great Templar castles as Safad and the Hospitaller stronghold of Krak des Chevaliers falling. The Pope, Clement IV, decided that a new crusade was called for, once the immediate problem of Sicily and Frederick's descendants had been dealt with. King Louis sent more money to the East via the Templars. No sooner had the funds been transferred, than further letters came from the East requesting more money to pay soldiers; appeals for help were unending. On 18 May 1268, Antioch fell and Thomas Bérard, the Templar Grand Master, decided that the Order's possessions in the Amanus March could no longer be successfully defended, and they were reluctantly abandoned. The seemingly unstoppable force of Baybars was only halted by the last crusade, that of Prince Edward of England, who persuaded the Mamluk sultan in April 1272 to agree to a ten-year truce. It was fortuitously timed. The Franks were in no position to hold out much longer, and Edward was forced to return to England upon the death of his father, Henry III, to assume the crown as Edward I.

At the Council of Lyons in May 1274, a new crusade was once again considered. Although the Templars played a prominent role in the talks – the Grand Master sat beside the Pope – an agreement could not be reached. Outremer was once again rent asunder by factional disputes, mainly centring around claims to the throne, with the Templars supporting Charles of Anjou, who had finally succeeded in wresting Sicily from the control of Frederick's son Conradin, whom he had had executed in Naples in 1268. Angry at what he saw as the Templars' adherence to no law save their own, the King of Jerusalem, Hugh III, simply upped and left for Cyprus, leaving no one in overall command. He tried to regain control of Outremer twice, in 1279 and 1283, but was unsuccessful on both occasions.

The Templars found themselves bogged down amid the various factions. They became involved in a civil war in the County of Tripoli between 1277 and 1282, an involvement that did nothing to enhance their reputation, and seems to have led to the Grand Master of the time, Guillame de Beaujeu, as being widely regarded as untrustworthy. Guillame did, however, get the Mamluks to agree to a new ten-year truce in 1282. In 1285, they broke it.

Baybars had died in July 1277, and his successor, Kalavun, was intent upon finishing the work that his predecessor had started. In April 1285, the coastal city of Latakia fell, followed by the Hospitaller fortress of al-Marqab the following month. The Templars were kept informed of Kalavun's plans by means of a double agent in the Mamluk hierarchy, and they were warned that Tripoli was in danger. Guillame sent a messenger to warn the Tripolitans, but, perhaps because of the Grand Master's apparent political duplicity, the message was not believed. In desperation, a second messenger was despatched, also to no avail. Once the Tripolitans finally realised they were in danger, it was too late for reinforcements to reach them, and the city fell to Kalavun in April 1289.

Letters to the West continued at a frantic pace. Finally, in August 1290, a fresh wave of crusaders landed at Acre. Unfortunately, they were the sort of crusader who would not have looked out of place on the First Crusade – they were by and large buccaneers, criminals and drunkards who wasted no time in causing a riot in which many Muslim traders were killed. This was the pretext that Kalavun needed for an attack upon the city. Once more, the Templars had advance warning courtesy of their well-placed source close to Kalavun, but again, like the boy who cried wolf, Guillame's warning was not believed.

On 5 April 1291, the Mamluks began their siege of Acre. Kalavun had died in November, but that had not stopped plans for an attack. His son, al-Ashraf Khalīl, assumed command. Ten days later, Guillame de Beaujeu led a daring night attack on al-Ashraf's forces, but the Templars were forced to retreat after becoming entangled in Mamluk tent ropes. On 15 May, a joint force of Templars and Hospitallers repelled a Mamluk assault on St Anthony's Gate, but were not able to keep the Muslim forces out indefinitely, and on 18 May, they broke into Acre at the so-called 'Accursed Tower'. Guillame de Beaujeu was apparently taking a well-deserved rest at the time, but, when he was told that the Mamluks were now inside the walls of the city, he rushed out into the mêlée without first stopping to put on all his armour. He was wounded in street fighting and died that evening. Within hours, the entire city apart from the Temple area was in Muslim hands and the harbour was full of ships taking refugees to Cyprus. On 25 May, the Templar Marshal, Peter de Sevrey, agreed to surrender if the Mamluks would guarantee the safety of all those who were taking refuge in the Temple compound. The Mamluks broke their word, but were beaten back by the Templars. There could now be no surrender. That night, the Templar Commander, Theobald Gaudin, sailed from Acre with the Templar treasure aboard his galley. Three days later, the Temple fell; everyone remaining inside fought to the death.

Theobald was elected Grand Master at Sidon by the remaining Templars there. A large Mamluk force appeared, and the Templars retreated to their stronghold. It was decided that Theobald would sail for Cyprus and bring back reinforcements. However, no reinforcements were forthcoming from Cyprus, only a message that it would be wise to leave the Holy Land; the Templars abandoned Sidon on 14 July. Haifa fell on the 30th, leaving only Tortosa and 'Atlīt in Templar hands. They were effectively cut off, and had no choice but to evacuate: Tortosa was abandoned on 3 August, and the impregnable 'Atlīt on 14 August. When the Mamluks reached 'Atlīt, they dismantled it for fear that the Templars should return and reoccupy the one castle that had defeated even Baybars. But their fears proved unfounded. When Acre fell, Outremer had fallen with it. The Templars would never return to the Holy Land.

Fall and Trial
(1291–1314)

Theobald Gaudin did not long survive the loss of Acre. He died on 16 April, either in 1292 or 1293, and was succeeded by the man who – along with Hugues de Payen – is perhaps the best known Grand Master of the Order, Jacques de Molay. Jacques was probably around 50 years old when he was elected to the position, almost certainly in a Chapter Meeting at the Order's new headquarters at Limassol on Cyprus. He had joined the Templars some three decades before, being initiated at Beaune in Burgundy in 1265 by Humbert of Pairaud, then Master in England, and Amaury La Roche, Master in France. From what is known about him, he appears to have been very much an 'old school' Templar, being a Master who was concerned solely with the restoration of Outremer, a position in marked contrast to that of the political machinations of Guillame de Beaujeu (but in fairness to Guillame, the Holy Land was still in Christian hands during his tenure as Master, and Molay faced a very different set of circumstances upon his accession to the post). Molay supported Pope Nicholas IV's calls for a new crusade, and much of his Mastership until 1307 was concerned with trying to re-establish a Frankish presence on the mainland (the only

Christian-held territory being the Templar garrison on the small island of Ruad, just off the coast from Tortosa).[27]

The Templars after 1291

With the seemingly only temporary loss of Outremer, talk was rife that the main military orders would have to merge, as the incessant bickering between the Temple and the Hospital was seen as one of the causes of the loss of the Holy Land. Neither order was keen on the idea, and the years immediately following 1291 saw the Templars, Hospitallers and Teutonic Knights trying to establish themselves in new territories and, in the case of the latter two orders, redefining their objectives. The Hospitallers cast themselves in a maritime role, making the Mediterranean their main sphere of operations. While initially based on Cyprus, in 1306 they invaded the island of Rhodes, making it their base three years later, a move that ensured them a relatively high degree of autonomy away from the interference of Rome and the kings of Europe. The Teutonics, meanwhile, decamped first to Venice and then to Marienburg in Prussia, where they devoted themselves entirely to the crusade against the pagans in the Baltic. Not only were they far away from Rome, they also fortified their position by the creation of Prussia as the *Ordensland*: this was literally a country created and run by a military order, something the Templars had long wanted to do.

The Languedoc had been the Templars' favoured location for a state of their own for some decades before the Fall of Acre, but they found themselves in the short term also on Cyprus. Although they had sold the island back to Richard the Lionheart in 1192, they had retained properties there, and Limassol became their new headquarters. However, the ghosts of the 1190s had not been entirely laid to rest, and the Order soon found itself enmeshed in local politics. King Henry of Cyprus was far from delighted to have the most powerful and feared military machine of the day arriving on his doorstep, and in 1298 he made an official complaint about the Templars' behaviour, citing the usual offences of arrogance and greed. In 1306 there was a coup, in which Henry was forced to abdicate in favour of his brother Amaury, who was supported by the Templars.

Jacques de Molay's first major undertaking as Grand Master was to travel to the West in 1294–95 to reinforce support for the Order. He arrived in Rome in December 1294, just as a new pope, Boniface VIII, was being invested. Boniface granted the Templars the same privileges in Cyprus as they had held in Outremer, which pleased Jacques de Molay, if not King Henry. Further help was at hand on the Italian peninsula: Charles II of Naples exempted the Order from paying taxes on exports of food. With such offers of help coming in, Jacques wasted no time in writing to every other monarch in Europe. He travelled to Paris and London, where Edward I promised that he would provide a crusading army once he had dealt with the French and the Scots. He also exempted the Order from paying export tax on funds that were going from the London Temple to Cyprus.

As with earlier crusades, the Templars played a central role in the build-up of a military presence in the East beginning in 1300. It was widely believed that the Mongols would return to the Holy Land, wrest Jerusalem from Mamluk control, and hand it back to the Franks. The Templars began to pave the way for a possible attack with a series of raids during the summer of 1300 on the coastal cities of Egypt and Syria, and in November they began preparations for an invasion of the mainland. Six hundred knights were sent to Ruad with orders to wait for news of the expected arrival of a combined force of Mongols under the Il-khan Ghazan and Armenians under King Hetoum. When the Mongols and Armenians did finally reach Tortosa in February 1301, they found no one there to greet them – with no sign of the reinforcements, the Templars had given up and gone back to Cyprus. To make the situation worse, the use of Ruad in this abortive campaign had alerted the Mamluks in Egypt to the strategic importance of the island, and, in 1302, the garrison there was wiped out by a Mamluk attack. It was the loss of the very last Templar holding in Outremer.

The Arrests

The spectre of merging the Temple with the Hospital returned with the investiture of Clement V as pope in November 1305. He invited both Jacques de Molay and Fulk de Villaret, the Grand Master of the Hospital, to write and explain their views on the matter. To Jacques de Molay, the idea was untenable. In his mémoire to the Pope, dictated in 1306, he examined the case for and against a merger, and concluded that the two orders, while having similar goals, would function better if they remained independent. Clement also requested de Molay's opinion on a new crusade, to which the Grand Master responded with a second mémoire. Crusades in the past had generally been either a *passagium generale*, where everyone was free to join, such as the First Crusade, or a *passagium particulare*, in which a limited number of professional soldiers would attack a specific target, which was usually the case with most of the later crusades. De Molay went against the prevailing opinion of the time and suggested that – given the loss of Ruad – the *passagium generale* was the only viable option. Clement was not convinced, and summoned both de Molay and de Villaret to France to meet to discuss the matter further. The meeting – planned for All Saints' Day 1306 – had to be postponed when the Pope suffered an attack of gastro-enteritis. De Molay arrived in the West in either late 1306 or early 1307. Fulk de Villaret, detained by the Hospital's campaigns on Rhodes, did not arrive until late summer.

It was while de Molay and Clement were waiting for the Hospitaller Grand Master to arrive in France, that a third matter was discussed: two years earlier, allegations of gross impropriety had been made against the Templars by several knights who had been expelled, and de Molay asked the Pope to look into the matter to clear the Order's reputation. On 24 August, the Pope wrote to the French king, Philip IV, stating that he could scarcely believe the accusations made against the Order, but, as he had heard many strange things about the Templars, had decided, 'not without great sorrow, anxiety and upset of heart'[28] to instigate an inquiry. He told Philip to take no further action.

But the French king did not listen. At dawn on Friday, 13 October, his agents arrested all the Templars then in France, including Jacques de Molay, who was seized at the Temple in Paris, on charges of heresy, sodomy, blasphemy and denying Christ.

The Trial

Philip's actions caused disbelief amongst the crowned heads of Europe. James II of Aragon was not alone in believing that the charges made against the Order were trumped up, in order for the notoriously insolvent Philip to get his hands on the Templars' vast wealth. It was not the first time the French king had shocked his contemporaries with his audacity and arrogance. In 1303, he had tried to kidnap the then pope, Boniface VIII, and bring him back to France to face charges similar to those levelled at the Templars; the attempt failed, but the shock killed Boniface. Philip also mounted a long-running campaign against the Italian bankers, the Lombards, finally arresting them and stripping them of all their assets in 1311. In July 1306, the Jews had been arrested, and all their wealth had been seized before they were thrown out of the kingdom. In addition, Philip had debased the coinage several times, which had proved highly unpopular. In 1306, he had had to take refuge in the Paris Temple to escape from an angry mob, and it is possible that it was while he was inside the Templar compound that he began to scheme of finding a way to appropriate their wealth to alleviate his own, seemingly never-ending, financial problems. By the time Clement wrote to Philip in August 1307, it seems that the French king's mind was already fully made up, and the instructions to arrest the Templars went out on 14 September.

That the main charge against the Templars should be heresy suggests that, for Philip, his campaign to eradicate the Order was a personal crusade which would put him on a par with his grandfather, Louis IX (whom Boniface VIII had declared a saint in 1297 at the French king's insistence). Philip was not only an arrogant bully, he was also fanatically religious, as was the other main figure behind the arrests, the Keeper of the Seals, Guillame de Nogaret. If anything, de Nogaret was even more of a zealot than Philip, and he is sometimes seen as the main instigator of the campaign against the Templars. (Interestingly, he is rumoured to have had a Cathar relative who died during the Albigensian Crusade – see below.) In the early fourteenth century, the fear of heresy and magic was real, and extended right the way through society, from peasants in their hovels to paranoid popes and kings. This is reflected in the heresy charges against Boniface – according to Philip and de Nogaret, the Pope was in league with the Devil – and the similar accusations levelled at the Templars.

Clement, although often seen as a weak pope who was a puppet of the French crown, did not, much to Philip's anger, comply with the campaign against the Templars. Indeed, Clement was outraged. As the Order was answerable only to Rome, Philip's action in arresting the Templars within his domains was illegal; not only that, but de

Nogaret at the time was excommunicate.[29] In an angry letter to Philip written on 27 October, Clement states that Philip has 'violated every rule' by arresting the Templars, which was a blatant 'act of contempt towards ourselves and the Roman Church'.[30] Clement's feeling that the Church itself was under threat became, for him, the real struggle that was now about to unfold.

Two days before Clement's letter to Philip, on 25 October, Jacques de Molay confessed before an assembly from the University of Paris that he had denied Christ and spat on the Cross. Other confessions followed from all the other senior Templars in captivity. There was scandal and outrage in Paris, with mobs showing their anger against the Order. This played into Philip's hands, and he renewed pressure on Clement to issue the command for Templars everywhere to be arrested. On 22 November, Clement finally acquiesced, and issued the bull *Pastoralis praeeminentiae*, which ordered the arrest of all Templars in Europe.

If Philip had hoped that other rulers would follow his example, he was very much mistaken. King James II of Aragon was incredulous, Edward II of England did as little as possible for as long as possible, in Germany there was widespread disbelief, and in Cyprus the charges were simply not believed at all. In Italy the situation varied from state to state: Naples and the Papal States acted at once, while in Lombardy, there seemed to be widespread support for the Order. Arrests were eventually made in all countries, but the success in extracting confessions depended upon whether the particular country or state allowed torture. Thus, in England and across the Iberian peninsula – where torture was either legally prohibited or used very reluctantly at the behest of Clement – very few confessions were elicited from captive Templars. In Naples and the Papal States, however, the Inquisition was allowed to use what was euphemistically known as 'ecclesiastical procedure'; the number of confessions here was, unsurprisingly, higher, although not as high as in France, where every Templar arrested – including de Molay – had been subjected to torture.

Templar confessions ranged in content, no doubt depending upon the extremities of torture applied. Most confessed to spitting, trampling and urinating on the Cross during their reception ceremony, and denying Christ on the grounds that he was a false prophet. (One Templar admitted that he had been told 'Put not thy faith in this [the crucifix], for it is too young.') The reception ceremony also included obscene kisses, usually on the navel and the base of the spine, although some confessed to kissing on the buttocks or penis. The words of consecration were said to have been omitted from the Mass. Most also confessed to worshipping an idol called Baphomet, which, depending on who was confessing at the time, was a severed head, or was one head with three faces; in other cases it was said to be the face of a bearded man, and in others, a woman or a cat. There were also admissions of having sex with demonic women, and even killing newborn children.

Clement insisted that the confessions should be heard before a Papal committee, and on 24 December, Jacques de Molay and other senior Templars appeared before it. Now seemingly safely out of the hands of Philip, de Molay retracted his confession on the grounds that he had only confessed in the first place after being tortured. The other Templars with him did likewise. Needless to say, this put a major spanner in the works of what Philip and de Nogaret had both hoped would be a swift and decisive campaign to eradicate the Order once and for all, seize its wealth and declare the French Crown the *de facto* leader of Europe and the Defender of the One True Faith.

Clement was not to be bullied, and in February 1308, suspended proceedings. Philip immediately approached doctors at the University of Paris to try to bolster the legal standing of the case for the prosecution. In their reply of 25 March, the doctors did not feel that Philip had much of a case. The King was becoming apoplectic. In May, he called a meeting of the Estates General in an attempt to win over the majority of public opinion. This too met with mixed success, and general public support for the Templars seemed to be growing alongside a distrust of the King.

Matters came to a head in June when Clement arrived at Poitiers to try to wrest control of the whole affair away from the French Crown and back into the hands of Mother Church. Philip sent 72 Templars to confess before him. On 27 June, Clement heard the confessions and agreed to set up two inquiries to handle the case: one would look at the Order as a whole; and the other would examine the case of individual Templars. That he was under virtual house arrest, with French troops sealing the town off, was without doubt a major factor in Clement's willingness to at last go along with Philip's wishes. The rest of the summer was spent in a whirlwind of bureaucracy, with summonses going out in order to get the two commissions up and running. Indeed, on one day in August, nearly 500 such letters were issued in a single day. De Molay and other Templar leaders, held at Chinon, retracted their retractions (no doubt after suffering further torture), and things at last seemed to be going Philip's way.

But it was not to be that easy. Collating all the evidence took far longer than expected, a fact which exasperated Philip, and the Papal hearings did not formally open until over a year later, on 22 November 1309. Jacques de Molay appeared before the committee on 26 November and expressed his wish to defend his Order, but felt unable to do so as he was a 'poor, unlettered knight'. Unlike the other military orders, which seemed to be much more in tune with the increasing legalism of the period, the Templars under de Molay had seemed blithely unconcerned with the changing political climate in the West, and as a result, had no legal counsel at their disposal, a fact which now appeared to be their undoing. De Molay gave further evidence two days later, and repeated that he felt unable to defend the Order. He also made a further gaffe when he announced that he would not talk to anyone but Clement in person, as he firmly believed that he could exonerate both himself and his Order with a personal appeal.

Philip's agents let imprisoned Templars know that their Grand Master had failed to defend them, in the hope that it would break their morale, and, for a while, the ploy seemed to work. However, when the hearings began again in February 1310, two Templars, Peter of Bologna and Reginald of Provins, both of whom had had legal training in the years prior to 1307, stepped forward and announced that they wished to defend their Order against all charges made against it. Philip had no choice but to allow the Templars to make their defence. On 1 April, they made a convincing case for the Order's innocence, with Peter of Bologna in particular making a powerful appeal that the Templars were not only innocent of all charges, but had been the victims of a cruel plot. He railed against the use of torture, which had merely given the Inquisitors the confessions they wished to hear (one Templar admitted that he would have even confessed to murdering God in order to stop his torments), despite the fact that they had been promised by Philip that no torture would be used.

In a move that recalled his coercion of Clement at Poitiers in June 1308, Philip now once more turned to outright bullying to get his way. On 11 May, with support growing among the imprisoned brothers for their defence, it was announced that 54 Templars who had retracted their confessions were to be burnt to death as relapsed heretics. The following day, 54 members of the Order went to the stake protesting their innocence as the flames wrapped around them. Reginald of Provins disappeared from prison, but just as mysteriously turned up again, while Peter of Bologna went missing and was never seen again. (He was probably murdered by Philip's henchmen.) The Order had no one left to defend it, and the Templar defence promptly collapsed.

The End of the Order

The Council of Vienne, which had been scheduled to meet in October 1310 in order to suppress the Templars, had to be postponed as there was still no sign of the Papal hearings coming to an end. Finally, on 5 June 1311, they did. The Council of Vienne finally began its sessions on 16 October 1311. The turn-out was low, partially due to bad weather and also due to the lack of decent accommodation in the town. After dealing with two other pressing matters – a new crusade and Church reform – the council turned its attention to dissolving the Templars. Rumour was rife that the Temple would mount a last-minute defence, and, much to everyone's surprise, seven fully armed knights who had evaded arrest four years earlier appeared to defend the Order. Clement asked the council if they should be allowed to do so, and the majority agreed that the knights should be allowed to speak.

Needless to say, Philip was enraged, and even Clement himself seems to have been surprised by the decision to let the Templars have their say. The Pope wanted to end the whole matter once and for all. Disease was by now rampant in Vienne, with several Church fathers having succumbed, and the thought of Philip putting in another appearance did nothing for the Pope's confidence. On 20 March, Philip and a small armed force did indeed arrive in Vienne, and the Pope knew that he had to act quickly. Two days later, in a secret consistory, Clement issued the bull *Vox in excelso*, which, while not finding the Templars guilty as charged, dissolved the Order forever, such was the shame and infamy that had been brought upon it. There was still dissent among the Church fathers, with the Bishop of Valencia declaring that the suppression of the Templars was 'against reason and justice'.[31] On 2 May, a second bull, *Ad providam*, was issued, which – against Philip's wishes – transferred the Temple's possessions to the Hospital. Four days after that, a third bull, *Considerantes dudum*, gave the provincial councils the power to decide the fate of individual Templars. The fate of the Order's leaders was reserved for Papal judgment alone.

Jacques de Molay and three other senior Templars remained in prison, awaiting the Pope's decision. In late December 1313, Clement finally set up a council to decide the fate of the four men. The cardinals appointed by the Pope called for a meeting of doctors of theology and canon law to decide the matter, and the council finally met in Paris on Monday, 18 March 1314. Facing the doctors alongside Jacques de Molay were Geoffroi de Charney, Preceptor of Normandy, Hugh de Pairaud, the Order's Visitor [ambassador] in France and Geoffroi de Gonneville, Preceptor of Aquitaine and Poitou. All were old men: de Molay was at least 70; de Pairaud and de Charney were in their 60s; while de Gonneville was probably still in his 50s. They were led out to a platform in front of Notre-Dame, where the sentences were read out. As all four men stood guilty of heresy, they were condemned to 'harsh and perpetual imprisonment'.[32] Hugh de Pairaud and Geoffroi de Gonneville accepted the sentence, and were led away to die miserably in jail.

At this moment, perhaps dreading the thought of being

reimprisoned (he had spent the last four years in solitary confinement), Jacques de Molay began shouting that he and his Order were innocent of all crimes, and he publicly retracted his confession. This astounded the cardinals and doctors, and they suddenly did not know what to do. After seven years of captivity, during which time he had consistently failed to defend his Order, Jacques de Molay's finest hour was suddenly at hand. He adamantly refused to confess his guilt. Geoffroi de Charney rallied to his Master, and likewise insisted on the Order's innocence. The two men were taken back to their cells while news of the unexpected turn of events was rushed to Philip. The King now had a legal and ecclesiastical emergency on his hands. He summoned the lay members of his Council and the matter was resolved. As the two Templars were insisting upon their innocence, they were guilty of being relapsed heretics, and there was only one punishment for that — death by fire.

At around the hour of Vespers, Jacques de Molay and Geoffroi de Charney were led out on to the Ile-des-Javiaux in the Seine. In front of a crowd who had gathered to watch the two Templars in their last moments, the Grand Master and the Preceptor were stripped to their shirts. Witnesses reported that both seemed very calm, almost glad that their torment was now over. As he was fastened to the stake, de Molay asked to be turned towards the cathedral of Notre-Dame, and that his hands be freed so that he could die in prayer. His request was granted. As the flames grew about him, de Molay is said to have once more protested his innocence and that of the Order, and he called both Clement and Philip to meet him before God within the year. (Philip may in fact have been watching from an upstairs window in the nearby palace.) Geoffroi de Charney likewise protested from the stake:

> 'I shall follow the way of my master
> As a martyr you have killed him
> This you have done and know not
> God willing on this day
> I shall die in the Order like him.'[33]

After nightfall, when the two men were dust and ash and the crowd had dispersed, a number of friars from the nearby Augustinian house and certain other people – who have never been identified – went to the place of execution and collected the bones of the two Templars, intent on preserving them as relics.

Templar Mysteries

The fact that the Templars fell from grace so spectacularly suggests that some of the wilder accusations against them may have had some basis in reality. While most commentators at the time and subsequently have seen Philip's avarice as the motivating factor behind his attack on the Order, there are those, such as the eminent mediaeval historian Sir Steven Runciman, who believe that there was some truth to the charges: 'It would be unwise to dismiss these rumours [of heresy] as the unfounded invention of enemies. There was probably just enough substance to them to suggest the line along which the Order could be most convincingly attacked.'[34]

If the end of the Order remains controversial, then its beginnings are equally shrouded in mystery and silence.

The Mystery of Templar Origins

The traditional picture that Hugues de Payen and Godfroi de St Omer presented themselves to King Baldwin II around the year 1119 with the suggestion that they form an order of nine knights who would protect pilgrims visiting the Holy Land derives from Guillame of Tyre (died c.1186), the first chronicler to mention the Order. Yet Guillame, like most mediaeval historians, is unreliable. He notes that the Council of Troyes was held in the ninth year of the Order's existence, which would mean that the Templars were possibly launched at the Council of Nablus in 1120, yet he also notes that they accepted no new members for the first nine years as well. As Fulk, Count of Anjou, is known to have joined the Order on his pilgrimage of 1120, this would push the foundation date of the Temple back to 1111. As Runciman notes, Guillame's dating is 'confused and at times demonstrably wrong'.[35]

If Guillame is confused, then he is not the only one. The other two chronicles dating from the late twelfth century – those of Michael the Syrian and Walter Map – disagree not only with Guillame, but also with each other. According to Michael the Syrian (d.1199), it was the King of Jerusalem who suggested to Hugues de Payen that he form a military order, and puts the initial membership at 30. Walter Map (d.c.1210) believed that the Order was founded by a knight from Burgundy called Paganus who defended pilgrims he saw frequently attacked at a horse-pool near Jerusalem. Despite his best efforts, the number of infidels grew and he was forced to seek extra recruits, with the knights subsequently being given lodgings near the Temple of the Lord, which could very well be the al-Aqsa mosque, sitting as it does at the southern end of the Temple platform.

There is a further hint that the Templars were in existence before their official founding date of around 1119. Five years previously, the Bishop of Chartres had written to

Hugh, Count of Champagne – himself either a founding Templar or at the very least one of the Order's first supporters – upon his return from his second visit to the East: 'We have heard that ... before leaving Jerusalem you made a vow to join the Militia of Christ, that you will enrol in this evangelical soldiery.'[36] As the phrase 'Militia of Christ' would also be employed by St Bernard in reference to the Templars, and given the close ties between Hugh, Bernard and the fledgling Order, it is this comment from the Bishop of Chartres that is perhaps the most persuasive evidence we have that the Templars – in one form or another – existed at least as early as 1114.

The air of mystery that surrounds the Temple's early years is compounded by the fact that the years before the Council of Troyes are the Order's least documented period. Indeed, they are hardly documented at all. The Templars themselves had no official records of their foundation, which is unusual for a religious order. There were no Western chroniclers in Outremer until the time of the Second Crusade, and, more remarkably, the King's chronicler, Fulk de Chartres, who was living in Jerusalem at the time of the Order's supposed foundation, does not mention them at all. There are only four documents existing prior to Troyes that mention the Templars, two of them making note of the Order in connection with the Hospital.[37] A later chronicle – that of Ernoul and Bernard the Treasurer – also suggests that there was some kind of close link between the two Orders. Interestingly, in this version, the Templars 'asked the king to give them his palace in front of the Lord's Temple'.[38] Indeed, recent research[39] seems to confirm that the Templars were initially given accommodation by the Augustinian Canons of the Church of the Holy Sepulchre, and that the buildings they occupied were part of the Hospital, which lay just to the south.

So if the Templars were originally based at the Hospital – and possibly as early as 1111 – what where they doing? Out of the four pre-1129 documents, none of them describes the Templars as protecting pilgrims. Could they have been simply providing security at the Hospital, or was something else going on? It has frequently been asserted[40] that the Templars were part of some grand design that was inaugurated with the First Crusade. While this cannot be proved, it cannot be disproved either. Sufficient gaps exist in the historical record to allow the Templars a more nebulous role than that with which they have been traditionally ascribed. Certainly there were shady characters whose names have not come down to us who were moving in the background in the early years of Outremer. Godfroi de Bouillon, for instance, was accompanied to the East by a group of anonymous advisers. The name is known of only one of them, Peter the Hermit. Peter was possibly linked to a mysterious group of monks who arrived on Godfroi's estates at Orval in the Ardennes sometime around 1090, having travelled en masse from Calabria in Italy. Peter is then thought to have become Godfroi's personal tutor, and, in 1095, was one of those who called for a crusade. (Indeed, Peter actually led the first band of crusaders to leave Europe.) When Jerusalem fell, Godfroi was offered the crown of Jerusalem by a group of mysterious nobles, who included 'a certain bishop of Calabria', and Godfroi then seems to have had an abbey built just outside the city walls, on Mount Sion. The resulting Order of Sion is one of the most obscure religious fraternities of the period, and it has been suggested[41] that it is from this group that the Templars derived.

Hugh, Count of Champagne, is an even more interesting figure than Godfroi. His departure for the East in 1104 seems to have been at the behest of a group of anonymous nobles, and it is possible that Hugh visited Outremer on some kind of fact-finding mission. By the time of his second visit in 1114, the Militia of Christ – quite possibly the Templars – had been formed. Although Hugh did not join immediately, he returned to France and donated land to St Bernard, who used it to found the new monastic house of Clairvaux. St Bernard later became the Templars' chief apologist in the West, and the Cistercians and the Templars expanded at an exponential rate, with Hugh supporting both Orders. Was Hugh working in accord with some larger plan? At the very least he seems to have been a man who was acutely aware of the zeitgeist of his time. And when he did officially join the Templars in 1125, he had to swear an oath of fealty – as would any new recruit to the Order – to his own vassal, Hugues de Payen. This is remarkable in itself, and could suggest that even at this early stage, there was a powerful mystique surrounding the Order, which its members seem to have actively encouraged.

The Temple and the Temple Mount

One tradition holds that while officially supposed to be protecting pilgrims, the Templars – or a group of them, at least – were involved in archaeological excavations that took place beneath the Temple platform, in what are known as Solomon's Stables. There had long been rumours that the treasure of the Second Temple, which was destroyed in the conflagration of 70 AD, was hidden beneath the Temple Mount, and it is possible that Hugues de Payen, the Count of Champagne and others knew of this and undertook to find it. Alternatively, the Order could have stumbled across something in the stables while carrying out alterations, as they were known to have done a great deal of building work around the al-Aqsa mosque, starting from the 1120s.

If the Order did indeed find something beneath the Temple Mount, what could it have been? Speculation has been rife (indeed, where the Templars are concerned, speculation is always rife) that they found one or more priceless relics, such as the embalmed head of John the Baptist, documents pertaining to the true origins of Christianity, and the Ark of the Covenant. Then again, maybe the treasure of the Second Temple was unearthed, which was known to have been comprised of gold and other precious metals and stones. That a major find of this sort could have occurred is not beyond the realms of possibility; after all, the scrolls discovered at Nag Hammadi and Qumran in the mid 1940s had lain untouched and well preserved for almost 2,000 years.

The Temple and the Grail

If there is one priceless relic with which the Templars are most closely associated, it is the Holy Grail.[42] In popular chivalric epics of the period, such as Wolfram von Eschenbach's *Parzival*, the Templars are portrayed as its guardians. (Another grail romance, the thirteenth-century French romance *Perlesvaus*, may have actually been written by a Templar, such is its attention to detail in regard to military matters.) But the most interesting connection between the Templars and the Grail is that the city in which they were officially launched, Troyes, is also the city in which the first grail romance was written, that of Chrétien de Troyes, who composed his *Conte del Graal* around 1180.

The strong connection between the Templars and the Grail does not, of course, bring us any closer to understanding what the Grail actually is. Traditionally seen as the cup used at the Last Supper, which also caught the blood of Christ at Calvary, the Grail can also be seen as a Christianisation of the Celtic myths of the Cauldron of Plenty, which is said to have granted fertility to the land and to have been an endless source of renewal. But in the hands of Chrétien, the Celtic story is merely the foundation to which he grafts new material. That he was writing in Troyes suggests that whatever new information he was privy to, it was quite possibly brought back to the city by Templars or those associated with the Order. A slightly later version of the Grail story, Wolfram von Eschenbach's *Parzival* (composed c.1220) makes this more explicit by setting some of his poem in the East (he personally visited

Outremer around 1200), and by peppering his text with esoteric references that can only have come about through contact with the more mystically inclined elements in the Muslim world.

The Temple and the Arab World

It was after the failure of the Second Crusade that rumours began to circulate that the Templars had deliberately sabotaged the Crusade through their treacherous alliances with the infidel. The anonymous Würzburg annalist believed that the Templars had accepted a massive bribe from Unur, the ruler of Damascus at the time of the campaign, to engineer the retreat which led to the failure of the crusade. Although accusations like these betray the usual inability of Western chroniclers to grasp the complexities of the situation in the East, where some form of accommodation between the Franks and Islam was a practical necessity, the Templars' reputation does seem to have been tarnished from this time on (at least in the eyes of their critics in the West).

As has been noted, the Templars often employed Muslim secretaries, and a number of the Order learnt Arabic. Similarly, they had an unpredictable, but sometimes close, relationship with the Assassins, who are often seen as the Islamic equivalent of the Templars. The Order also came into contact with the Sufis. It is not beyond the realms of possibility, therefore, that ideas from the Islamic world found their way back to Europe via the Order. Twelfth-century Moorish Spain, for instance, also acted in this way, with a vast amount of learning coming into Europe via places like the University of Toledo, which had a school entirely devoted to translating works from the Arabic. This influx of knowledge had an incalculable effect on the West; indeed, it would not be too much of an over-statement to suggest that one of the most important things in the intellectual development of the West was the discovery of the East, Arabic culture and science being far in advance of the West at this time. It is this close contact with the Arab world that may have contributed to the alleged religious heterodoxy of the Templars.

The Temple and Heresy

Religious heterodoxy nearer home may also have been tainting Templar thought. The Order has long been associated with the Cathars, the heretical dualist sect which flourished in the twelfth and thirteenth centuries, mainly in southern France and parts of northern Italy. Alarmed at the spread of the heresy, Pope Innocent proclaimed a crusade against it, which got under way in 1208 under Simon de Montfort. This was the so-called Albigensian Crusade, named after the French town of Albi. It was to last on and off until 1244, when the last Cathar stronghold at Montségur fell to the forces of Louis IX and its occupants were burnt to death on the Field of the Cremated. While the majority of Templars would have been simple, unlettered men who adhered to the Catholic Church, there were elements within the Order who would have certainly been sympathetic to Catharism. Bertrand de Blancfort, the sixth Grand Master of the Temple, was from a Cathar family, and the Order welcomed Cathars into its ranks once the Albigensian Crusade was under way. So great was the number of Cathar Templars in the Languedoc that, in many preceptories, Cathars outnumbered Catholics. The Order had always accepted excommunicates into its ranks – the reason for this being usually cited as the constant manpower shortage in the East – but the same cannot be said for the Order's sheltering of Cathars in the West, where the manpower situation was nowhere near as dire. This apparent friendliness towards the Cathars could be a legacy of Bertrand de Blancfort, and it could have also led to the Order's consideration of the Languedoc – where the Templar presence was particularly strong – as the most likely site for the creation of their own *Ordensland*.

Catharism was not the only heresy with which the Order has been associated. The other most prominent is the Johannite heresy, the belief that John the Baptist is the real Messiah, with Christ being seen as a usurper and a false prophet. It has been suggested that Hugues de Payen himself was a Johannite, and the Order are known to have held John the Baptist in particularly high regard. The origins for this are obscure, but one possible source could be the Templars' putative original base in the Hospital: around 1100, the Hospitallers, originally known as the Hospital of Jerusalem of John the Almoner, became – for reasons unknown – the Hospital of Jerusalem of John the Baptist.

Closely associated with the Johannite movement is the cult of Mary Magdalene. The cult of the Virgin Mary was also at its height in the twelfth century, and the two women are traditionally seen as the feminine face of God. St Bernard himself was obsessed with the Divine Feminine, and, given his close relationship with the Templars, may have either transmitted a reverence for the Feminine to the Order, or developed his fascination at the same time as certain other members of the Templars. One must not forget also that Europe at this time was undergoing rapid changes (the so-called Renaissance of the twelfth century), and it is a curious fact that explosions of interest in the Goddess tend to recur at times of great change and enquiry. So, this begs the question: were the Templars secret Goddess worshippers?

Pope Innocent III certainly thought that they were worshipping something other than the God of the New Testament and his only Son, when he admonished the Order in his letter of 1208. He accused them of the usual sins of pride and arrogance – accusations that date back at least as far as the Second Crusade, when rumours of the Order's alliance with Islam were also beginning to circulate – but also branded them as necromancers who were in danger of doing the Devil's work unless they got their house in order. That the Pope himself should be moved to admit that there was something altogether not quite right about the Templars suggests that rumours of the Templars being tainted with heresy may well have had some basis in fact.

The Head of the Templars

Charges of Devil worship notoriously resurfaced a century later, during the Order's trial at the hands of Philip IV. This seven-year period is possibly the best documented in the Order's history, and it is also the one period in which their alleged unorthodox beliefs were at the centre of interest. The French prosecutors homed in on two areas of Templar practice: the initiation ceremony; and the fact that they were supposed to worship an idol named Baphomet.

At the initiation ceremony, it was alleged, the new brothers had to show their loyalty to the Order by spitting, trampling or urinating on the Cross, and by denying Christ. These have traditionally been seen as another example of Philip's trumped-up charges. But the recent discovery in the Vatican Library of what is known as the Chinon Parchment suggests that the Templars did indeed spit on the Cross and deny Christ. Under questioning at Chinon in the summer of 1308, Jacques de Molay explained that these apparently sacrilegious practices were designed to get a Templar to experience the sort of torture he would likely receive at the hands of the Saracens, and thereby enable them to deny their religion 'with the mind only and not with the heart'.[43] When one recalls that some of the evidence against the Templars was collected by 12 of Philip's spies, who joined the Order in 1306 to substantiate the allegations made the year before by the expelled knight Esquin de Floyran, it suggests that the charges against the Order were in fact true, but the purpose of these ceremonies had been misunderstood by Philip's men.

Misunderstanding is almost certainly at the root of the allegation that the Templars worshipped an idol called Baphomet. Descriptions of it varied, but it was usually described as being a life-sized head, which was said to make the land fertile (as is said of the Grail). That the Templars did possess heads is without doubt. They possessed the head of St Euphemia of Chalcedon at their preceptory in Nicosia on Cyprus, and, more curiously, a silver head-shaped reliquary was found after the arrests at the Paris Temple. This bore the inscription CAPUT LVIII, and inside it were parts of a woman's skull (who was believed to have been one of the 11,000 virgins martyred at Cologne with St Ursula). The heads may have indeed been worshipped, in the way that the Celts revered the head. The Assassins, during their initiation ceremonies, buried the initiate up to his neck in sand, leaving only the head visible, before disinterring him. Given their simulation of Saracen torture, the Templars may also have carried out this practice. A further possibility is that Baphomet, long thought to be a mistranslation of 'Mahomet' (the Prophet Muhammad), could well be a corruption of the Arabic word *abufihamat*, which means 'Father of Understanding', a reference to a spiritual seeker after realisation or enlightenment has taken place: 'The Baphomet is none other than the symbol of the completed man.'[44] It is therefore possible that the supposed head the Templars worshipped was actually a metaphorical head. That Hugues de Payen's shield carried three black heads suggests that certain elements within the Order – the upper echelons perhaps – were involved with esoteric disciplines learned from the Sufis from the very beginning of the Temple's existence.

The Templars after 1314

The eminent nineteenth-century Catholic theologian and historian Ignaz Dollinger was once asked what he thought was the most evil day in history. He did not hesitate in his reply: it was Friday, 13 October 1307, the day the Templars were arrested in France.[45] The feeling that the arrests were a criminal act of unparalleled dimensions were felt at the time. Dante compared Philip IV to Pontius Pilate and charged him with avarice in the *Purgatorio* (Canto XX), and the subsequent myths surrounding the Templars got off to a very quick start – Clement died only a month after Jacques de Molay had called him to account before God within the year, and Philip himself died on 29 November 1314.

Although the trial and suppression had succeeded in destroying the Order of the Temple, it failed in other areas. Philip did not find the Templars' treasure, and most of the Order's lands ended up being passed on to the Hospital. It is also unclear just how many Templars were actually arrested (the figures range between 2,000 and 15,000), and it is likewise uncertain as to how many escaped. Certainly the Order seems to have received some kind of tip-off – shortly before the events of 13 October, Jacques de Molay recalled all the Order's rule books and accounts and had them burnt. A brother who left the Order in 1307 was told that he was 'wise', as an unspecified catastrophe was looming. A memo was circulated to all French preceptories forbidding them from releasing any information about the Order's rites and rituals.[46]

If the Order knew what Philip's plans were in advance, that might explain why the French king was unable to find the Order's treasure (assuming it to have been actual, rather than metaphorical), which was said to have been smuggled out of the Paris Temple shortly before the arrests and taken by river to the Templars' main naval base at La Rochelle. How many Templar ships sailed from La Rochelle in the autumn of 1307 is unknown – what they were carrying likewise – but one thing is known: the Templar fleet vanished utterly.

If the Order did indeed have some kind of advance warning, and an unknown number of Templars escaped, where did they go to? Although the Order of the Temple ceased to exist in 1312, Templars did not, and various theories have been proposed as to their subsequent fate. Some were welcomed into the Hospital, while others joined the Teutonic Knights. Templars in Portugal actually went nowhere – King Diniz found the Order innocent of all crimes, and the Templars there simply changed their name to the Knights of Christ. Under this name, they continued for another two centuries, and were heavily involved in exploration. Prince Henry the Navigator and Vasco da Gama were both Knights of Christ, as was Christopher Columbus's father-in-law; it is possible that the rumours that the Templars discovered America originated with the exploits of these Knights of Christ. In Spain, likewise, the Order of Montesa was created 'primarily as a refuge for fugitive Templars'.[47]

The fate of the Templar fleet has never been resolved. Almost the only place the ships could have found a safe haven would have been western Scotland, then under the control of Robert the Bruce. This theory is explored at length by Michael Baigent and Richard Leigh in their book *The Temple and the Lodge*, which proposes that a contingent of Templars landed in Argyll, helped Bruce to win the Battle of Bannockburn and then continued to reside in Scotland relatively unmolested. (All the Scottish Templars escaped arrest.) These Templars, and spin-off orders such as the Scots Guard, helped to pave the way for the emergence of Freemasonry. Eighteenth-century Freemasons were quick to capitalise on their supposed Templar ancestry.

If Scotland, at odds with both England and the Papacy, could have offered a safe haven for a group of Templars, then the emerging country of Switzerland could have provided another. One theory has been put forward[48] that a group of Templars became involved with the struggle for Swiss independence sometime after the first three Cantons – Uri, Schwyz and Unterwalden – signed a pact of mutual assistance in 1291. Swiss folk tales tell of white-clad knights appearing to assist the Cantons in the struggle against the Holy Roman Empire; the date is also significant, as, after 1291, the Templars were seemingly without a raison d'être for their continued existence. Whether or not these knights – assuming they were Templars – saw the emerging Swiss confederacy as a potential *Ordensland* of their own is impossible now to determine, but two factors lend credibility to this thesis. Firstly, the Swiss, once established, suddenly acquired, as if from nowhere, the best army in Europe. Their military prowess would remain unchallenged until the Battle of Marignano in 1515, when they were comprehensively defeated by the French. Secondly, Switzerland is famous (or infamous, depending upon one's point of view) for its banks. The Templars were the true originators of the international banking system that is still in use today, predating the great Italian houses by more than a century. Perhaps it is this that is the Templars' main legacy to us. As Desmond Seward notes, 'no mediaeval institution did more for the rise of capitalism'[49] than the Templars.

A Fable Agreed Upon

The Templars are inseparable from their myth. Such is the strength of this myth that it sometimes appears that each writer who deals with them is seemingly writing about a different Order, from the academics who maintain that the Templars were, in reality, very ordinary men, to the more speculative camp who portray the Order as a secret society of mystical initiates. Ever since the time of Cornelius Agrippa, who wrote in his *De occulta philosophia* (1531) that the Templars committed 'detestable heresy',[50] the reality of who the Templars actually were and what they actually did has been ever more obscured by later generations of commentators. The eighteenth-century Masonic movement, with its neo-Templar affectations (including the so-called Strict Templar Observance form of Freemasonry) has done much to muddy the waters. There were claims that the Order was still in existence in the early nineteenth century, and a highly suspicious list of post-1314 Grand

Masters was produced by the Freemasons (see Appendix II).

As Michael Baigent and Richard Leigh point out,[51] the two camps tend to remain firmly apart, as, on the one hand, academic historians will only consider whether something 'actually happened', and which can be backed up by documentation and other forms of evidence, while the more speculative apologists for the Order thrive on the mythical side of the Templars. What Baigent and Leigh point out is that something does not have to 'actually happen' in order for it to become subsumed into the collective consciousness and affect later generations. For a myth that can affect history, one need look no further than the myth of Aryan supremacy, which the Nazis held to be gospel, with such catastrophic results. What continues to fascinate about the Templars is this apparent dichotomy between the reality and the myth, and it can only be possible to understand the Order as a whole if the mythical aspect is also considered alongside the facts.

Umberto Eco points out[52] that the conspiracy theorists tend to project a great deal of their own failings into their theories, no matter how wild. What he does not examine, however, is that the hands that write the more standard, orthodox history, can also be driven by similar forces: the desire for peer acceptance; the desire to maintain one's position within academe; and, perhaps more importantly, one's funding, all of which would be severely compromised by entertaining the more mythical version of the Templar story. This latter approach ignores anything vaguely speculative about the Order, and, in doing so, perpetuates a blinkered and restricted view of history.

As the great Tibetan saint Padmasambhava once said, 'Things are not what they seem; nor are they otherwise.' That the Order, even in its own time, was fanatically secretive only compounds the difficulty of arriving at anything close to a definitive account. It would be plausible to argue, therefore, that the Templars were, in the main, very ordinary men, but that certain elements of the Order were indeed 'tainted'. Whether we will ever know by what, is, of course, another matter, and whether recent discoveries such as the Chinon Parchment force us to re-evaluate our thinking about the Templars, one thing remains certain: the mystique and fascination of the Order of Poor Knights of Christ and the Temple of Solomon will continue to exert their hold, and the aura surrounding the Order will continue, maybe deepen even further, and perhaps never be fully fathomed. The mystery will remain.

Endnotes

See also the Bibliography.

1 Baigent, Leigh & Lincoln, *The Holy Blood and the Holy Grail* (Jonathan Cape, 1982), p.51.

2 Genesis 22:12–18.

3 Daniel, 'The Life and Journey of Daniel', in *Jerusalem Pilgrimage*, ed. J. Wilkinson, Hakluyt Society 167 (London, 1988). Quoted in Barber, *The New Knighthood* (Cambridge University Press, 1994), p.3.

4 Daniel, *ibid.* Quoted in Barber, *op. cit.*, p.6.

5 St Bernard, from a letter to Pope Calixtus II, 1124/5. Quoted in Barber, *op. cit.*, p.13.

6 All of these knights were among the original nine members. According to Barber (*op. cit.*, p.12), King Baldwin had already sent two of the original nine Templars, André de Montbard and Gondemar, to France for Church approval of the Order. This would leave only the unknown ninth member (Hugh of Champagne?) in Outremer, reinforcing the theory that the Templars – in order to be taken seriously by Baldwin II, the Pope and the Council of Troyes – had to be more than nine knights strong by 1129.

7 Guigo, Lettres des Premiers Chartreux, *Sources Chrétiennes* 88, Paris 1988. Quoted in Barber, *op. cit.*, p.49.

8 Barber, *op. cit.*, p.42.

9 Quoted in Read, *The Templars* (Weidenfeld & Nicholson, 1999), p.119.

[10] Barber, *op. cit.*, p.230.

[11] R.C. Smail, *Crusading Warfare, 1097–1193* (Cambridge, 1995), p.43.

[12] Theodericus, ch.17, pp.26–7 in *Jerusalem Pilgrimage*, pp.293–4; quoted in Barber, *op. cit.* pp.90–93.

[13] Genesis 32:24–29.

[14] Read, *op. cit.*, p.155.

[15] Read, *ibid.*, p.158.

[16] Quoted in Barber, *op. cit.*, p.115.

[17] Barber, *ibid.*, p.116.

[18] Gestes des Chiprois, pp.252–3; quoted in Barber, *op. cit.*, pp.241–3.

[19] Seward, *The Monks of War* (Penguin Books, 1992), p.37.

[20] The connection between Lazarus and leprosy is a mysterious one. Lazarus, in John's Gospel, did not suffer from the disease. It is possible that the Templars used Lazar houses for purposes other than that of treating lepers, knowing that fear of the disease would mean that the houses would remain undisturbed.

[21] Barber, *op. cit.*, p.64.

[22] For a treatment of children raised in silence, see John Burnside's novel *The Dumb House* (Cape, 1997); for the search for the language of Eden, see Umberto Eco's *The Search for the Perfect Language* (Blackwell, 1997).

[23] Some chronologies list Richard de Bures as the Grand Master between Armand and Guillame. As no list of Grand Masters is definitive, we can assume that either Richard actually was the head of the Order between La Forbie and Guillame de Sonnac's election in c.1247, or that he was acting as a caretaker Grand Master who would have stepped aside had Armand de Périgord emerged from captivity or until a successor could officially replace him.

[24] Barber, *op. cit.*, p.152.

[25] Quoted in Read, *op. cit.*, p.228.

[26] *Flores Historiarum* (London, 1890); quoted in Barber, *op. cit.*, p.157.

[27] Although the Fall of Acre is usually seen as the end of the Christian presence in the East, there was one remaining Christian stronghold in mainland Syria after 1291, the Templar castle of La Roche Guillame, in the Amanus March, which held out against all odds until 1299. See Malcolm Barber and Keith Bate, *The Templars: Selected Sources* (MUP, 2002), p.15.

[28] Barber, *The Trial of the Templars* (Cambridge University Press, 1978), p.48.

[29] A result of de Nogaret's attempts to kidnap Boniface VIII at Agnani in September 1303.

[30] Quoted in Read, *op. cit.*, p.265.

[31] Quoted in Read, *op. cit.*, p.295.

[32] Edward Burman, *Supremely Abominable Crimes* (Allison & Busby, 1994), p.266.

[33] Burman, *ibid.*, p.272.

[34] Sir Steven Runciman, *A History of the Crusades*, Vol. III, p.435–6.

[35] Runciman, *ibid.*, Vol. II, p.477.

[36] Baigent, Leigh & Lincoln, *op. cit.*, p.57.

[37] Barber, *The New Knighthood*, p.8.

[38] Helen Nicholson, *The Knights Templar: A New History* (Sutton, 2001), pp.29–30.

[39] Barber & Bate, *op. cit.*, p.2.

[40] e.g. Baigent, Leigh & Lincoln, *op. cit.*, pp.35–65, pp.81–100, in particular pp.62–5.

[41] Baigent, Leigh & Lincoln, *op. cit.*, pp.81–8.

[42] They are also associated in some quarters with the Turin Shroud. See Keith Laidler, *The Divine Deception* (Headline, 2000), and Christopher Knight & Robert Lomas, *The Second Messiah* (Random House, 1997). Interestingly, the first family to exhibit the supposed shroud was the de Charneys, related to the Preceptor of Normandy who died with de Molay at the stake.

[43] 'Vatican File Shows Pope Pardoned Massacred Knights', *The Times*, 30 March 2002.

[44] Idries Shah, *The Sufis* (Octagon Press, 1964), p.226.

[45] Quoted in Mark Hedsel, *The Zelator* (Random House, 1998), p.131.

[46] Michael Baigent & Richard Leigh, *The Temple and the Lodge* (Jonathan Cape 1989), p.84.

[47] Baigent & Leigh, *ibid.*, p.88.

[48] Alan Butler & Stephen Dafoe, *The Warriors and the Bankers* (Templar Books, 1998).

[49] Seward, *op. cit.*, p.222.

[50] Quoted in Peter Partner, *The Murdered Magicians* (OUP, 1981), p.92.

[51] Baigent & Leigh, *op. cit.*, pp.127–31.

[52] Umberto Eco, *Foucault's Pendulum* (Secker & Warburg, 1989), p.619.

[53] Baigent, Leigh & Lincoln, *op. cit.*, pp.413–4.

Appendix I:
Chronology

c.1070	Birth of Hugues de Payen; Foundation of the Hospitallers
1095 (November)	Pope Urban II calls for a crusade to recapture Jerusalem
1099 (July)	Jerusalem captured by the First Crusade
1104	Hugh of Champagne arrives in Outremer (possibly with Hugues de Payen)
1114	Bishop of Chartres refers to a military order called the 'Militia of Christ'
c.1119	Traditional founding date of the Templars
1120 (January)	Council of Nablus: Templars accepted in the East
1127	First meeting between Hugues de Payen and St Bernard of Clairvaux
1129 (January)	Council of Troyes. The Latin Rule of the Temple established
1131	*In Praise of the New Knighthood* by St Bernard
1135	Earliest records of Templars acting as bankers
c.1136	Death of Hugues de Payen (possibly 1131); Hospitallers begin militarisation
1136–37	Templars first established in the Amanus March
1139	*Omnes datum optimum* (possibly as late as 1152)

1144	*Milites templi* (possibly as early as 1134)
1145	*Militia Dei*
1147–49	The Second Crusade
1148–49	Templars granted Gaza
1153	Fall of Ascalon to the Franks
Mid 1160s	Hierarchical statutes or *retrais* added to the Rule
Late 1160s	Statutes on conventual life, the holding of chapters, and penances added to the Rule
1168	Templars refuse to participate in the Egyptian campaign
1173	Assassin envoy murdered by the Templars
1187 (1 May)	Battle of the Springs of Cresson
(4 July)	Battle of Hattin
(2 October)	Jerusalem falls to Saladin
1188	Council of Gisors: the 'Cutting of the Elm'
1189–92	The Third Crusade
1192	Templars move headquarters to Acre
1191–92	Templars occupy – and for a short time, own – Cyprus
1191–1216	Templars and Leo of Armenia in conflict over the Amanus March
1198	Foundation of the Teutonic Knights
1202–04	The Fourth Crusade
1208	Innocent III accuses the Templars of necromancy; Start of the Albigensian Crusade
1217–21	Building of the castle of 'Atlīt (Pilgrim's Castle)
1218–21	The Fifth Crusade
1228–29	Crusade of Frederick II
1239–40	Crusade of Theobald of Champagne
1240–41	Crusade of Richard of Cornwall
1240	Rebuilding of Safad begins
1241–42	Siege of the Hospital compound at Acre

1243	Eviction of Imperial forces from Tyre
1244 (16 March)	Fall of Cathar stronghold at Montségur
(23 August)	Loss of Jerusalem
(17 October)	Battle of La Forbie
1248–54	Crusade of St Louis
1250 (8 February)	Battle of Mansurah
1257–67	Additional clauses on penances added to the Rule
1266	Fall of Safad to the Mamluks
After 1268	Catalan Rule of the Templars
1271–72	Crusade of Edward of England – truce negotiated with Mamluks
1274	Council of Lyon
1277	Maria of Antioch sells her rights to the throne of Jerusalem to Charles of Anjou
1277–82	Civil War in Tripoli
1291 (May)	Fall of Acre to the Mamluks
(August)	Templars evacuate Tortosa and 'Atlīt
1299	Fall of La Roche Guillame
1300	Templars attack Egyptian coastal towns
1300–01	Abortive attempt to retake the Holy Land
1302	Loss of Ruad and massacre of the Templar garrison
1305	First allegations made against the Order by Esquin de Floyran
1306	Templars support Amaury in coup in Cyprus; Jacques de Molay returns to the West
1307 (13 October)	Arrest of the Templars in France
(19 October)	Parisian hearings begin
(24 October)	Jacques de Molay's first confession
(22 November)	*Pastoralis praeeminentiae* calls for Templars everywhere to be arrested

(24 December)	De Molay retracts his confession before Papal committee
1308 (February)	Clement suspends proceedings
(27 June)	72 Templars confess before Clement
(August)	Papal Commissions launched; De Molay interviewed at Chinon
1309 (22 November)	Papal commission begins its proceedings
(26 & 28 November)	De Molay appears before commission
1310 (April)	Templar defence begins
(10 May)	Burning of 54 Templars as relapsed heretics near Paris
1311 (5 June)	Papal hearings finally end
(16 October)	Council of Vienne begins
1312 (22 March)	*Vox in excelso* abolishes the Temple
(2 May)	*Ad providam* transfers Temple property to the Hospital
(6 May)	*Considerantes dudum* allows provincial councils to judge cases
1314 (18 March)	Burning of Jacques de Molay and Geoffroi de Charney
(20 April)	Pope Clement V dies
(24 June)	Battle of Bannockburn
(29 November)	Philip the Fair dies
1319	*Ad ea exquibis* recognises the Knights of Christ
1571	Presumed destruction of the Templar archive on Cyprus by the Ottomans

Appendix II:
Grand Masters of the Temple

There is no definitive list of Templar Grand Masters. If one ever existed, then it is possible that it was amongst the documents destroyed by Jacques de Molay shortly before the arrests of 1307. The earliest known list dates from 1342.

c.1119–c.1136	Hugues de Payen
c.1136–c.1149	Robert de Craon
c.1149–c.1152	Everard des Barres*
c.1152–1153	Bernard de Tremelay
1153–1156	André de Montbard*
1156–1169	Bertrand de Blancfort
1169–1171	Philip de Nablus*
c.1171–1179	Odo de St Amand
1181–1184	Arnold of Torroja
1185–1189	Gerard de Ridefort
1191–1192/3	Robert de Sablé
1194–1200	Gilbert Erail
1201–1209	Philip de Plessis
1210–1218/19	Guillame de Chartres
1219–1230/32	Peter de Montaigu
c.1232–1244	Armand de Périgord
c.1244–c.1247	Richard de Bures*
c.1247–1250	Guillame de Sonnac
1250–1256	Reginald de Vichiers
1256–1273	Thomas Bérard

1273–1291	Guillame de Beaujeu
1291–1292/93	Theobald Gaudin
c.1293–1314	Jacques de Molay

*Disputed.

Many Grand Master lists omit Richard de Bures (see Note 23, above).

The Masterships of Everard des Barres and André de Montbard have been called into question by Baigent, Leigh and Lincoln in *The Holy Blood and the Holy Grail*.[53] As regional masters and Grand Masters often signed themselves as '*magister templi*', it has often led to confusion about precisely who was Grand Master and who was merely a regional master.

All the Masters died in office, with the exception of Everard des Barres, who resigned to become a monk at Clairvaux, where he was still living in 1176, and Philip de Nablus, who apparently also resigned. While Hugues de Payen died in his bed, other Masters were not so lucky: Bernard de Tremelay died during the siege of Ascalon; Gerard de Ridefort at Acre; Guillame de Sonnac at Mansurah; Guillame de Beaujeu during the Fall of Acre; Jacques de Molay was executed as a relapsed heretic. Odo de St Amand and Armand de Périgord both died in Muslim jails.

Gilbert Erail was the only Grand Master to be excommunicated (later rescinded by Pope Innocent III).

In the nineteenth century, a Masonic document surfaced claiming to list all the Grand Masters of the now-underground Templar movement, starting with Jean-Marc Larmenius, who is alleged to have taken over from Jacques de Molay in 1314. It is generally regarded as extremely spurious, and is not quoted here.

Appendix III:
The Charges Against the Templars

Although by June 1308 127 charges had been made against the Templars, the initial charges of the previous October fall into these nine basic categories:

1. That during the reception ceremony, new brothers were required to deny Christ, God, the Virgin or the Saints on the command of those receiving them.
2. That the brothers committed various sacrilegious acts – trampling, spitting, urinating – either on the Cross or on an image of Christ.
3. That the receptors practised obscene kisses on new entrants, on the mouth, navel, base of the spine or buttocks.
4. That Templar priests did not consecrate the host, and that the brothers did not believe in the sacraments.
5. That the brothers practised idol worship of a cat or a head, called Baphomet.
6. That the brothers practised institutional sodomy.
7. That the Grand Master, or other high-ranking officials, absolved fellow Templars of their sins.
8. That the Templars held their reception ceremonies and Chapter meetings in secret and at night.
9. That the Templars abused the duties of charity and hospitality and used illegal means to acquire property and increase their wealth.

For an exhaustive study of the trial, see Malcolm Barber, *The Trial of the Templars* (Cambridge University Press, 1978). Edward Burman's *Supremely Abominable Crimes* (Allison & Busby, 1994) focuses on the Paris hearings of 1310.

Barbara Frale's book on the Chinon Parchment, which should throw considerable new light on the trial, is forthcoming.

Bibliography

Orthodox

Malcolm Barber, *The Trial of the Templars* (Cambridge University Press, 1978); *The New Knighthood: A History of the Order of the Temple* (Cambridge University Press, 1994)

Malcolm Barber & Keith Bate (translators & editors), *The Templars: Selected Sources* (Manchester Medieval Sources Series, Manchester University Press, 2002)

Edward Burman, *Supremely Abominable Crimes: The Trial of The Knights Templar* (Allison & Busby, 1994); *The Templars: Knights of God* (Inner Traditions, 1990)

Helen Nicholson, *Templars, Hospitallers and Teutonic Knights: Images of the Military Orders* (Leicester University Press, 1993); *Love, War and the Grail: Templars, Hospitallers and Teutonic Knights in Medieval Epic and Romance, 1150–1500* (Brill, 2000); *The Knights Templar: A New History* (Sutton, 2001)

Peter Partner, *The Murdered Magicians* (Oxford University Press, 1981)

Piers Paul Read, *The Templars* (Weidenfeld & Nicholson, 1999)

Desmond Seward, *The Monks of War: The Military Religious Orders* (Penguin Books, 1992)

Judi Upton-Ward (trans.), *The Rule of the Templars: The French Text of the Rule of the Order of Knights Templar* (Boydell Press, 1992)

Speculative

Michael Baigent, Richard Leigh & Henry Lincoln, *The Holy Blood and the Holy Grail* (Jonathan Cape, 1982)

Michael Baigent & Richard Leigh, *The Temple and the Lodge* (Jonathan Cape, 1989)

Françine Bernier, *The Templars' Legacy in Montreal, the New Jerusalem* (Frontier Sciences Foundation, 2002)

Alan Butler & Stephen Dafoe, *The Warriors and the Bankers* (Templar Books, 1998); *The Templar Continuum* (Templar Books, 1999)

Erling Haagensen & Henry Lincoln, *The Templars' Secret Island* (Weidenfeld & Nicholson, 2002)

Christopher Knight & Robert Lomas, *The Second Messiah* (Random House, 1997)

Keith Laidler, *The Head of God: The Lost Treasure of the Templars* (Weidenfeld & Nicholson, 1998); *The Divine Deception* (Headline, 2000)

Jean Markale, *The Templar Treasure at Gisors* (Inner Traditions, 2003)

Lynne Picknett and Clive Prince, *The Templar Revelation* (Bantam, 1997)

Karen Ralls, *The Templars and the Grail* (Quest Books, 2003)

Andrew Sinclair, *The Sword and the Grail* (Century, 1993); *The Secret Scroll* (Sinclair Stevenson, 2001)

Related Interest

W.B. Bartlett, *The Assassins: The Story of Islam's Medieval Secret Sect* (Sutton, 2001)

Nigel Bryant (trans.), *The High Book of the Grail: A Translation of the Thirteenth-Century Romance of 'Perlesvaus'* (D.S. Brewer, 1978)

Edward Burman, *The Assassins* (Crucible, 1987)

E. Christiansen, *The Northern Crusades: The Baltic and the Catholic Frontier 1100–1525* (Macmillan, 1980)

Umberto Eco, *Foucault's Pendulum* (Secker & Warburg, 1989)

Wolfram von Eschenbach, *Parzival* (Trans. AT Hatto Penguin Books, 1980)

Malcolm Godwin, *The Holy Grail* (Bloomsbury, 1994)

Joinville & Villehardouin, *Chronicles of the Crusades* (Penguin Books, 1963)

Helen Nicholson, *The Knights Hospitaller* (Boydell, 2001)

Mike Paine, *The Crusades* (Pocket Essentials, 2001)

Jonathan Riley-Smith, *The Knights of St John in Jerusalem and Cyprus 1050–1310* (Macmillan, 1967)

The Oxford Illustrated History of the Crusades (Oxford University Press, 1995)

Sir Steven Runciman, *A History of the Crusades* (3 Vols) (Penguin Books 1990–91)

Yuri Stoyanov, *The Other God: Dualist Religion from Antiquity to the Cathar Heresy* (Yale University Press, 2000)

Idries Shah, *The Sufis* (Octagon, 1964)

William Urban, *The Teutonic Knights: A Military History* (Greenhill Books, 2003)

William Watson, *The Last of the Templars* (Harvill, 1978)

Internet

www.templarhistory.com